Chiara Berlendi

The Role of Social Media within the Fashion and Luxury Industries

Chiara Berlendi

The Role of Social Media within the Fashion and Luxury Industries

Depicting Social Media's possible role within the peculiar communication strategy carried by a Fashion or Luxury company

LAP LAMBERT Academic Publishing

Impressum/Imprint (nur für Deutschland/ only for Germany)

Bibliografische Information der Deutschen Nationalbibliothek: Die Deutsche Nationalbibliothek verzeichnet diese Publikation in der Deutschen Nationalbibliografie; detaillierte bibliografische Daten sind im Internet über http://dnb.d-nb.de abrufbar.

Alle in diesem Buch genannten Marken und Produktnamen unterliegen warenzeichen-, marken- oder patentrechtlichem Schutz bzw. sind Warenzeichen oder eingetragene Warenzeichen der jeweiligen Inhaber. Die Wiedergabe von Marken, Produktnamen, Gebrauchsnamen, Handelsnamen, Warenbezeichnungen u.s.w. in diesem Werk berechtigt auch ohne besondere Kennzeichnung nicht zu der Annahme, dass solche Namen im Sinne der Warenzeichen- und Markenschutzgesetzgebung als frei zu betrachten wären und daher von jedermann benutzt werden dürften.

Coverbild: www.ingimage.com

Verlag: LAP LAMBERT Academic Publishing GmbH & Co. KG
Dudweiler Landstr. 99, 66123 Saarbrücken, Deutschland
Telefon +49 681 3720-310, Telefax +49 681 3720-3109
Email: info@lap-publishing.com

Herstellung in Deutschland:
Schaltungsdienst Lange o.H.G., Berlin
Books on Demand GmbH, Norderstedt
Reha GmbH, Saarbrücken
Amazon Distribution GmbH, Leipzig
ISBN: 978-3-8443-9379-8

Imprint (only for USA, GB)

Bibliographic information published by the Deutsche Nationalbibliothek: The Deutsche Nationalbibliothek lists this publication in the Deutsche Nationalbibliografie; detailed bibliographic data are available in the Internet at http://dnb.d-nb.de.

Any brand names and product names mentioned in this book are subject to trademark, brand or patent protection and are trademarks or registered trademarks of their respective holders. The use of brand names, product names, common names, trade names, product descriptions etc. even without a particular marking in this works is in no way to be construed to mean that such names may be regarded as unrestricted in respect of trademark and brand protection legislation and could thus be used by anyone.

Cover image: www.ingimage.com

Publisher: LAP LAMBERT Academic Publishing GmbH & Co. KG
Dudweiler Landstr. 99, 66123 Saarbrücken, Germany
Phone +49 681 3720-310, Fax +49 681 3720-3109
Email: info@lap-publishing.com

Printed in the U.S.A.
Printed in the U.K. by (see last page)
ISBN: 978-3-8443-9379-8

UNIVERSITA' COMMERCIALE "LUIGI BOCCONI"
Graduate School in Business and Economics
Master of Science in Economics and Management of Art Culture Media and Entertainment

The Role of Social Media within the Fashion and Luxury Industries.

Advisor:

Prof. Stefania **SAVIOLO**

Discussant:

Prof. Erica **CORBELLINI**

Master Thesis of:

Chiara BERLENDI

ID 1359348

Academic year 2009/2010

Ringraziamenti

Sono davvero moltissime le persone a cui devo un Grazie per la serenita', l'affetto e l'aiuto che mi hanno saputo dare e dimostrare in questi ultimi due anni - e questo non perche' io sia affetta da 'Ringrazite', come sostiene mio Zio Tiziano.

Il primo Grazie va senz'altro alla mia Famiglia, a Mamma e Papa', per l'Amore, la fiducia ed il sostegno costante, per aver creduto in me e avermi dato la possibilita' di arrichire il mio percorso scolastico ed universitario con esperienze che, mi rendo conto, non sono purtroppo alla portata di tutti; e a Maria, la mia fantastica sorella, esempio vivente del 'volere è potere', per le interminabili chiamate su skype e messagini su Facebook. Mi mancate tutti e tre tantissimo.

Grazie alla mia seconda Famiglia: alla mia Nonna Dina - che si preoccupa ogni 'tre per due' per la sua nipotina, per il buon senso, i preziosi consigli e le coccole infinte - e ai miei Zii Tiziano ed Anna Maria, che hanno sempre viziato me e mia sorella fino all'inverosimile, per avermi regalato un'infanzia piena di bei ricordi e per avermi insegnato cosa significa 'farsi il mazzo' pur continuando a coltivare i piccoli piaceri della vita. Forse non lo sapevate, ma vi ammiro e stimo tutti e tre.

Grazie alla mia Famiglia allargata, a tutte le mie Bellissime Cugine e al Cugino, agli Zii, al Nonno e a chi nel frattempo non c'e' piu'- ma, chissa' - per le iniezioni e le ricariche di Gioia e Allegria;

Grazie ai miei stupendi Amici, quelli del Triennio che sono rimasti, vicini e lontani – you guys know who you are! – e quelli nuovi del Biennio che si sono aggiunti, tra lavori di gruppo e stage, per le grasse risate, il conforto ed il supporto quotidiani.

Grazie alla Professoressa Stefania Saviolo, che mi ha permesso di concludere il mio percorso universitario trattando l'argomento che piu' mi appassionava, per i consigli concisi ma decisivi, per la sua disponibilta' e doti umane.

Infine - *last but not least,* come dicono gli inglesi - Grazie a te Fulvio, per la spensieratezza, la dolcezza e l'Amore che mi hai saputo regalare in questi quattro anni, per la giocosita', la complicita' e, non è poco, per avermi ridato fiducia verso il prossimo.

Table of Contents

Abstract

This thesis was aimed at depicting Social Media's possible role within the peculiar communication strategy carried by a Fashion or Luxury company.

While the recruitment of Social Media within a firm's media plan is today nearly considered a 'routine activity' in the vast majority of sectors, the same cannot be asserted for what concerns Social Media's adoption by industries where the Value Chain is greatly influenced by the interaction between economics, management and creative and intellectual attributes.

In fact, for what concerns these sectors, the adoption of these latter has been very recent and has developed exponentially only within the last couple of years.

This brought us to the following research question: "Are Social Media the new essential tool to be paired with 'Old Media' (the press) for a Fashion or Luxury company to implement a successful communication strategy?".

To test this hypothesis, six different real initiatives, carried by six different companies pertaining to either the Luxury or Fashion (both low and high end) sectors have been reported and analyzed. The acclaimed discretion that these industries apply to their numbers and other types of data impaired the possibility to carry a respectable quantitative analysis. The conclusions were hence mainly drawn by the study of the six cases and supported in part by some unofficial numbers - meaning that these data were not disclosed directly by any of the companies mentioned - retrieved by reliable sources such as Audiweb, the Social Media Monitoring program 'Scoutlabs' and reports from the consulting companies Nielsen and McKinsey.

The analysis derived from this combination of information brought a positive answer to our initial research question. The thesis' conclusion highlights Social Media main upsides, regardless of the industry adopting them, and humbly proposes some rules of thumb for their implementation.

Introduction

This thesis aims to illustrate how Social Media has become, within a few years, a very important (if not indispensable) tool for any business striving to achieve a complete and comprehensive communication strategy. In particular, it will focus on firms competing in the Fashion and Luxury industries. In fact, the hypothesis that this paper wishes to test is the following: "Are Social Media the new essential tool to be paired with 'Old Media'[1] for a fashion or luxury company to implement a successful communication strategy?".

Given my ever-present interest and curiosity towards the sector of Fashion and Luxury, I thought it would be interesting to analyze the behavior of certain companies competing in this very peculiar arena. I already knew (from personal experience and thank to the courses that I attended in these years at Bocconi University), that this type of firms had a very unique way of running a communication strategy.

Things got even more interesting when these latter started using the so-called 'Social Media' to advertise and promote their brands. The employment of Social Media by Fashion and Luxury companies for the boosterism of an event, product or collection has been plain to see, and not only because financial magazines such as the Financial Times or the Wall Street Journal were writing about it. One could actually verify this occurrence by surfing the Web. There, for anybody to see, are Luxury and Fashion brands' official blogs; also Twitter and Facebook are loaded down with these brands (such as Roberto Cavalli, Bulgari, Burberry or Valentino). Some others, like Dolce and Gabbana, Louis Vuitton or Gucci are broadcasting their shows live on the Internet[2]. Since this has been going on for nearly two years now, can we still talk about Fashion and Luxury brands 'testing' Social Media applications to see what kind of benefits they engender?

Wouldn't it be more appropriate to state that Fashion and Luxury companies have recognized and acknowledged Social Media as an advantageous tool for the fostering of their Brand Image?

---

[1] Intended as the press
[2] Bulbarelli, P. (2009). *Milano, moda e tecnologia a braccetto*. Corriere della Sera's article.
http://www.corriere.it/spettacoli/speciali/2010/moda/notizie/moda-tecnologia-sfilate-diretta-web_16d945d2-20bf-11df-a848-00144f02aabe.shtml

These are some of the questions at the basis of this project. My thesis indeed aspires to identify, and hopefully clarify, whether Social Media have a role within this kind of company's communication strategy, and whether their role is a crucial one.

While I have found some reliable books and papers that explain the peculiar structure of a fashion and luxury's company's communication strategy, there are very few that mention Social Media; the great majority doesn't in fact mention them at all.

This knowledge gap can be easily explained by the fact that authoritative reading material on Social Media - as a broad subject - is being finally published only now, even if we have been talking about it for a certain time. While conducting my search for trustworthy material on which to base my thesis, I was indeed amazed by the enormous quantity of books that have been published last year and this year alone (2009-2010) only to define what Social Media is. I hence stumbled across a wide variety of sources, but very few concerned the Fashion and Luxury sectors. This is perhaps due to the fact that we will have to wait a little bit longer for more in-depth and specific literature on this subject matter – for instance, on how Social Media's use may vary across different industries. The fact that fashion and Luxury firms are using Social Media as part of their communication strategy is however verifiable the observation of real cases – this is indeed the path I undertook with my work.

My thesis thus intends to describe and analyze how, following a general trend: Fashion and Luxury companies have started using Social Media within their communication strategy, even though Social Media's main characteristic - their ability to democratize anything they 'touch' - clashes in a very evident way with fashion and luxury's communication strategy's main feature – exclusiveness; in which way their adoption has to be carried to achieve overall effectiveness and, most important of all, whether, in this sector in particular, the lack of use of Social Media is still excusable or not.

My work is hence split up into four chapters. The First one aims to define in a simple but exhaustive way the framework within which Social Media are likely to be inserted: the Communication Strategy adopted by a Fashion or Luxury company. This is indeed where Social Media are most likely to have a significant effect since they are first and foremost a communication tool. The chapter will continue with an explanation of Fashion and Luxury sectors' main peculiarities.

The Second chapter defines what Social Media is, from both an etymological and a historical point of view as well as explaining their main features – and in which way they may enhance (or not) the overall communication strategy.

In the Third chapter I bring, as empirical evidence, the examples of some Fashion and Luxury companies that have started to use Social Media in their communication strategy. In the Fourth chapter I carry an analysis of the factors that could lead to a successful or unsuccessful use of Social Media within the Fashion and Luxury industry, taking as references the cases introduced in chapter Three. This last chapter will result from a comparison between the existing literature on Social Media, reported in chapter Two, the cases I described in chapter Three and some additional quantitative data.

I hope that this thesis will be relevant in pointing out how Fashion and Luxury communication departments can profit from Social Media to strengthen their Communication Strategy in order to bring it to a new level.

Chapter One: Fashion and Luxury companies' Communication Strategy

Social Media are a tool aimed at improving society's communication. They are therefore likely to be firstly used and have a significant effect within a firm's communication department. Let us hence specify the main features characterizing the Fashion and Luxury's one.

Paragraph 1.1: Fashion and Luxury companies' communication strategy's characteristics.

Communication is crucial as it is what transforms the luxury or fashion product into a brand. The product on its own indeed incorporates only the tangible dimension of Fashion goods – products produced with high quality materials by skilled craftsmen. What generates the idea of a lifestyle? What creates the dream factor that characterizes the offering of Fashion and Luxury companies? How is the product presented to possible consumers? The answer to all of these questions is a properly implemented communication strategy (high impact, universal and consistent). Without it, there wouldn't be sustenance for symbolic contents.

Fashion companies build their communication strategy on a variety of tools such as catwalk shows, celebrities marketing, product placements – always very connected with aspirational & contemporary lifestyles – and the use of advertising space on fashion magazines. Of course, Luxury companies also use these tools, but seldom and with a higher degree of exclusiveness.

This means that a key aspect in the communication strategy of a fashion brand is visibility, which is achieved through very vast communication investments and the predominance of visual elements (such as images, photos or videos over words) – the former having the undeniable quality of universality. Fashion companies spend huge amounts of money: to set up a catwalk show (the average cost for one fashion show being $/€ 300,000[3]), to secure the most sought after fashion photographers and models for their campaigns, to assure the celebrity of the moment for their celebrity endorsement, to buy as much advertising space as possible in the first pages of fashion most glossy magazines and to get the highest impact locations to set up their flagship and directly operated stores.

Magazines in particular, with their editorials and commercials, account for 60% of communication investments, because they enhance *product communication,* the most important form/level of communication for a Fashion company. In these sectors, the communication process is indeed simultaneously carried also at the *brand* and *corporate* levels by the communication department.

Carrying the communication process at three different levels concurrently is a first peculiarity of fashion and luxury companies. This is in fact the only way to manage and achieve Brand Awareness (the brand is known and well recognized by competitors thanks to product communication), Brand Image (the brand is associated with certain specific values thanks to brand communication) and Brand Reputation (a good brand reputation, gained through corporate communication, is indeed necessary to attract banks and private equity investments) all at once[4]. This is the second peculiar characteristic of a fashion or luxury's communication strategy: achieving Brand Image, Awareness and Reputation all at the same time.

Other communication tools adopted are television commercials (product communication), events – for instance, Dolce and Gabbana's presentation of their first fragrance collection for women at the Milanese department store 'La Rinascente' in September 2009[5] – (product communication), official web sites (brand communication), the set up of a foundation or charity (corporate communication), the disclosure of a spokesperson's interview (brand communication), the organization of

[3] Olins, A. and Bannerman, L. (2009). *New York Fashion Week to host catwalk show without the catwalk.* Newspapers' article. Times publications.
http://women.timesonline.co.uk/tol/life_and_style/women/fashion/article5622399.ece
[4] Corbellini, E. & Saviolo, S. (2009). *Managing Fashion and Luxury Companies.* 1st Edition. Milan. Etas. Chapter 13.
[5] *Naomi, Eva e Claudia: la moda fa spettacolo.* (2009). Newspapers' article. Il Corriere della Sera publications.
http://archiviostorico.corriere.it/2009/settembre/26/Naomi_Eva_Claudia_moda_spettacolo_co_7_0909263069.shtml

an exhibition, such as the ones dedicated to Ferragamo in 2009[6] and to Armani[7] in 2007 at the Triennale of Milan (corporate communication) or the opening of a new flagship store, which in emerging country is a successful example of brand communication[8].

This preponderance of images has to be consistent across the whole company as well as outside of it. For this reason, the designer holds nearly any kind of decision making for what regards this matter, so as to promote an overall harmony[9].

Luxury companies, on the other hand, build their communication strategy almost exclusively on a specific key characteristic: the dream factor. They must ensure that the audience perceives the brand as something they passionately aspire to, as something they fantasize about and set their hearts after. In other words, the brand must be what they 'dream of'. The difficulty here is to balance the idea of exclusiveness and uniqueness of the offer with the idea that the product can be, after all, reached. The dream factor shouldn't dissuade consumers from buying the luxury product; on the contrary, it should persuade them to buy it.

Hence, luxury brands can deploy the same tools used in a fashion company's communication strategy, such as events, the purchase of advertising space on fashion magazines, catwalks – if the company offers a clothing line – but with a higher level of exclusiveness. Cartier for instance doesn't use fashion shows as it does not have an apparel line and Louis Vuitton started only in 1997[10].

The persuasion is achieved by leveraging on certain aspirational factors in possible luxury consumers. Classic tools to achieve this aim are storytelling and a successful

[6] Fontanelli, R. (2008). *Web, accessori e design le tre sfide di Ferragamo*. Newspapers' article. La Repubblica's online database.
http://ricerca.repubblica.it/repubblica/archivio/repubblica/2008/10/27/web-accessori-design-le-tre-sfide-di.html
Mostre – archivio La Repubblica dal 1984. Internet source
http://ricerca.repubblica.it/repubblica/archivio/repubblica/2008/11/02/mostre.html
[7] Cirillo, A. (2007). *Armani, un regalo a Milano*. Newspapers' article. La Repubblica's online database. http://ricerca.repubblica.it/repubblica/archivio/repubblica/2007/02/20/armani-un-regalo-milano.html
[8] Corbellini, E. & Saviolo, S. (2009). *Managing Fashion and Luxury Companies*. 1st Edition. Milan. Etas. Chapter 5 p.90
[9] 'Valentino, the Last Emperor' – movie http://www.valentinomovie.com/
[10] Schiro, A.M. (1997). *Designers' Council Opens Door a Bit*. The New York Times's artcile. http://www.nytimes.com/1997/12/09/style/designers-council-opens-door-a-bit.html.
Louis Vuitton official international website. Heritage section, Timeline.
http://www.louisvuitton.com/en/flash/index.jsp?direct1=home_entry_gb0

management of brand heritage[11]. Luxury companies in particular are at least one century old[12]; they thus have a considerable wealth of experiences from which to draw strength. Hence, luxury houses use communication to reinforce the brand heritage, the dream of the brand and their iconic products. The latter is also strengthen by the wide offering that generally characterizes Luxury companies: Hermès for instance, has as many as 14 different product categories[13], offered to its clients to make sure that they experience the Brand 'Lifestyle'.

Fashion companies' communication strategy is therefore more 'democratic', in the sense that it favors equality (it is not as exclusive as) when compared to the one implemented by luxury companies.

Paragraph 1.2: Fashion and Luxury companies' communication department.

The communication department carries the communication strategy/plan. Within a luxury and fashion's company there is, in general, one department only that takes care of the three different types of communication processes. The latter implements a strict supervision, both internal and external, to coordinate the work of the many professionals with very diverse backgrounds working within and with the company to make sure that they all share the same vision, that of the firm.

Within the communication department, the two most important bodies are perhaps the Press Office and Public Relations office. These are the translation of the obsessive attention to details that characterizes Fashion companies.

1. The former takes care of managing images and video archives, of issuing and distributing new press releases, of building and keeping contacts with international, national, local and industry press and of monitoring and measuring media coverage results, in terms of quality (possible positive or

[11] Corbellini, E. & Saviolo, S. (2009). *Managing Fashion and Luxury Companies*. 1st Edition. Milan. Etas. Chapter 10.
[12] Cartier, for instance, was founded in 1847.
Cartier's official website. *Living Heritage, Through Time*. http://www.cartier.us/#/tell-me/living-heritage/through-time?selectedYear=1847:/tell-me/living-heritage/through-time/1847
[13] Rinaldi, F. & Raviolo, S. (2008/2009). *Business Models in Fashion and Luxury*. Bocconi Graduate School cases.

negative articles/references by the media) and quantity (the number of times a certain message has been sent out) in order to generate corrective actions when necessary[14].

2. The latter tracks all the public actions of a brand, organizes the presentation of a sample collection or the opening of a new boutique, launches a new line, manages relationship with key clients and takes care of celebrity dressing (the gifting or lending of certain branded products to celebrities, on the occasion of certain important events)[15].

The Public Relations office is hence the 'organ', within the communication department of a Fashion brand, endowed with the duty of talking to a competent audience, to be used in order to set up and maintain an important network of relationships among all the persons with an interest in the brand business (i.e. the different stakeholders). Its job is that of influencing the opinion leaders working in the Fashion industry. If positively impressed, they will participate in diffusing a positive image of the brand, thereby helping its building process. This is a peculiarity of high-end fashion brands' public relations offices: they mainly target individuals working in the industry – e.g. it-girls, famous journalists, heads of buying of the most famous fashion department stores, stylists, creative directors, managers, designers and their family members. The influencing of the public opinion happens only in a second moment. Public relations office's role is crucial: it guarantees the creation of the so-called 'word-of-mouth' between 'those that count', an essential ingredient of the recipe for the eligibility of a company.

Obviously, the more a Fashion company tends to be qualified as a Mass Fashion company, the less it will focus on brand or corporate communications. However, it still will spend a considerable amount of money for the product communication, so as to increase its overall brand awareness; it will focus on advertising the attributes and benefits of its products rather than the intangible and visual characteristics; it will invest largely to find a very good store location, but in terms of traffic – the more the movement of pedestrians, the better – rather than in terms of prestige; it will use promotions and sponsorships instead of catwalk shows – one of the main reason

---

[14] Corbellini, E. & Saviolo, S. (2009). *Managing Fashion and Luxury Companies*. 1st Edition. Milan. Etas. Chapter 13 p.233
[15] Corbellini, E. & Saviolo, S. (2009). *Managing Fashion and Luxury Companies*. 1st Edition. Milan. Etas. Chapter 13 p.235

being that fashion shows are the celebration of *the designer*, of the lifestyle he/she promotes, of its role as a spokesperson; but mass brands generally have a group of individuals working as designers (e.g.: American Apparel, H&M or Zara).

The communication strategy adopted by low-end brands is therefore quite different if compared to that of highly successful fashion designer's brands. Other dissimilarities are the fact that the latter basically never rely on advertising agencies or media centers, which are unable to provide the right degree of personalization required and that mass fashion brand make a wide use of promotions[16].

The last important difference is that Mass Fashion brands have been the first to use the so-called 'interactive' media. Maybe because they could not afford to buy much advertising space on fashion magazines or because they were among the first to realize that advertising is more and more costly and not always functional[17], mass fashion brands have turned their attention towards web related communication means.

As different as these communication strategies can be (in particular if we compare the one adopted by Mass Fashion brands with the one of Luxury brands), they are all set up in accordance with the overall Brand strategy (intended not as the brand communication strategy but as the brand's/firm's overall strategy, which is affected by the firm target audience, its current or possible competitors and the threat of new entrants or new substitutes/ rival products). For any Fashion or Luxury company, the communication strategy is moreover carried in five steps, by the communication director in accordance with the CEO, the designer and with the help of his/her peers (and in some cases his/her subordinates).

In step One, they must decide *who* is to be targeted with the communication strategy to be created. 'To whom is it addressed?' This is the key question to be answered during this first step. If the communication strategy to come is more focused on advertising a certain product, it will probably target with greater attention existing and possible clients/consumers; if it is more focused on communicating a corporate aspect, it will target with greater awareness existing or possible new financial investors.

---

[16] Corbellini, E. & Saviolo, S. (2009). *Managing Fashion and Luxury Companies*. 1st Edition. Milan. Etas. Chapter 13, p. 226.
[17] Ferdi, D. & Serlenga, L. (2008). *Alla corte di re Moda*. 1st Edition. Milan. Salani Editore.

As aforementioned, the peculiarity of Fashion and Luxury's communication strategy is that it is carried at three different levels simultaneously (product, brand and corporate).

In step Two, the communication director will probably consult the marketing director and the retail one too to decide how to carry the communication strategy. In particular they must agree on the key message to communicate (how to word it accurately, emphasizing what, etc.) and on the type of communication channels to be used.

This means deciding the media planning for the communication strategy to come, i.e. which communication tools and methods would it be more advisable to use; old media like the press? Television? Events? The Internet and the new media? All of them? Once the media plan is decided, it will be the task of the Press Office and of the Public Relations' one to implement it.

In step Three, presumably with the help of the chief financial officer, the budget is decided. A limited budget will obviously require a certain prioritization of the goals and objectives to be reached with the communication.

In step Four, the timetable, the calendar marking all the important tasks is set up and responsibilities are assigned.

In the Fifth and last step, measurements and adjustments are addressed. Evaluation procedures must be set up to test the communication strategy planned until now to see if it performs correctly (does it reach the right goals with the amount of resources planned?). If it does not, it has to be adjusted to reduce the variance between foreseen and observed results as much as possible.

Paragraph 1.3: Why is the use of social media by fashion and luxury companies seen as controversial?

We have just described how a Fashion or Luxury communication department is likely to be structured and how it is likely to operate while setting up the communication strategy. Within this framework then, where are Social Media supposed to fit? The answer is: within the media plan.

What also showed through the previous explanation was that there is another main feature shared by plus or minus any Fashion or luxury communication strategy:

Exclusiveness. Curiously enough though, both types of company (as we will see in Chapter Three) have adopted Social Media as a communication tool. This is very unexpected of Luxury and High-end Fashion companies, as Social Media, according to the definition we will provide in Chapter Two, tend to dilute exclusivity – one of the key features of Luxury companies.

Isn't it therefore questioning, to say the least, that these companies have adopted Social Media, even though *their* main feature clashes in an evident manner with the selectiveness of a fashion and luxury's communication strategy? Social Media indeed allow the sharing of any kind of information with anybody. They are hence inclusive rather than exclusive, democratic rather than selective.
Still, what started off as – and was labeled by many – a 'temporary' phenomenon is definitely gaining ground. While skeptics are still wondering why and how this is possible, those who have accepted this evidence are meanwhile trying to understand *what* renders Social Media so useful for a Fashion and Luxury company to use them permanently and which extra or bonus characteristics do Social Media have with respect to Traditional media.
Indeed, when Social Media started to become popular, many welcomed them as *substitutes* of Old Media. And here arises the main and sole controversy regarding these tools: should they be inserted in the media plan so as to substitute old media (the press) or should they not be introduced at all, since they have been labeled 'a temporary phenomenon'?
How come there are such diverse opinions on this subject matter? Who is more likely to be in the wrong?

Following this logical path I ended up with the subsequent Research Question:
"Are Social Media the new essential tool to be paired with 'Old Media' for a Fashion or Luxury company to implement a successful communication strategy?".
This question, is dissimilar from, for instance: "Are Social Media as essential and necessary as Old media within a fashion and luxury's communication strategy?". In the sense that the former not only aims to prove that Social Media *should* be inserted in a fashion or luxury communication strategy, but that they *must* be part of it, for the latter to be successful.

Chapter Two: What are social Media.

As mentioned in the introduction, I was amazed, while conducting my search for trustworthy material, by the enormous quantity of books that have been published last year and this year alone (2009-2010) only to define what Social Media is. Before the internship that I undertook last autumn, I myself had a very vague idea of what "Social Media" was, or at least I was unable to provide an exhaustive and complete definition when asked to. I quickly discovered that I was not alone: far too many did not know what terms such as "Web 2.0" meant. And I am not referring only to my relatives or friends who might have no interest in keeping up to date with the fast growing array of internet-generated communication tools: many professionals still do not know how to properly define Social Media.

The great majority of people working in a business of any kind, collaborating with co-workers and peers to solve problems, creating systems, services or products to make their company more competitive and valuable do not have a clear idea of what Social Media is.

Lon Safko, one of the authors of the most complete book on social media (The Social Media Bible: Tactics, Tools, and Strategies for Business Success, 2009), admits that when he started researching for his book by interviewing and consulting more than 1,000 professionals he found out that *'out of more than 1,000 surveyed, two-third did not know what it was, but nearly 100 % knew that social media was going to affect them and their business'*[18].

Paragraph 2.1: A first attempt at defining Social Media.

A first attempt to define Social Media may arise from the etymological understanding of these two words, 'Social' and 'Media' [19]. While Social Media is a phrase made of two very familiar words, the meaning of this sentence itself is very *unfamiliar* to many people.

---

[18] Safko, L. & Brake, D. K. (2009) *The social media bible: tactics, tools, and strategies for business success*. 1st Edition. Hoboken. John Wiley & Sons. p.XV.
[19] Definition retrieved from the New Oxford American Dictionary.

Media (noun), plural of medium, are the main means of mass communication – whether we are referring to the television, the radio, newspapers or the internet– regarded collectively. The word media comes from the Latin plural of 'medium' dating back to the late 16th century and originally denoting something intermediate in nature or degree- literally 'middle'; media are indeed 'in the middle' between the source issuing a certain information and the audience who is waiting to receive it.

The traditional view is that it should therefore be treated as a plural noun in all its senses in English and be used with a plural rather than a singular verb. For instance "the media *have* gone too far" (rather than: *has* gone).

In practice, media – in the sense of television, radio, the press, and the **Internet**– behaves as a collective noun (like *staff* or *clergy*, for example), which means that it is now acceptable in standard English for it to take either a plural or even a singular verb. While the latter usage may still result fastidious for some, it must be accepted.

Social (adjective) portrays a relationship with society or its organization. It originates either from old French 'social', or from Latin *socialis* – literally meaning '*allied*'.

From this first etymological analysis, we can easily guess that 'Social Media' is indeed the communication means our society converses with.

Following this explanation, newspapers, television, radio and the telephone, for instance, are all likely to be defined as Social Media.

This statement is however slightly inaccurate. While it is certainly true that the television, the radio and newspapers are all communications means with which our society transmits and shares content, it must also be admitted that nowadays these are not what we refer to – or most simply what one has in mind – when talking about Social Media.

On Wikipedia [20] for instance, Social Media is defined as "*online practices and technologies that users adopt to share content, feelings, opinions, experiences, and the same media*".

The key word here is 'online'. This is what makes the difference. These days, when we talk about Social Media, we mainly – if not exclusively – refer to *online* technologies, to *online* communication means. It is no exaggeration to state that the vital element for the creation of Social Media was undoubtedly Internet.

---

[20] www.wikipedia.com

The following paragraph is hence aimed at defining the Internet and in which ways it is dissimilar from the 'Web'.

Paragraph 2.2: Internet and the World Wide Web.

The Internet is a web of interconnected devices, a network of computers, a 'network of networks' made of private, public, academic, business, and government networks, with local or global scope, linked by a vast assortment of electronic and optical networking technologies.

Created in 1987, Internet is the result of the work of the Defense Advanced Research Project Agency (DARPA) implemented by The Pentagon in the eighties. The first 'ancestor' of Internet as we know it today can indeed be defined as a network of electronic calculators connected with each other (interconnected) to cover the entire country; a 'network of fine threads' – labeled DARPAnet or ARPAnet – where all components were equivalent one to the other and autonomous one from the other; a web designed for military forces to exchange related data and information.

The World Wide Web is the main 'format' with which we share information *over* the Internet, through the use of hypertext. In other words, the World Wide Web (commonly known as 'the web') "*is a system of interlinked hypertext documents accessed via the Internet*" [21]. So, if the Internet is a 'network of computers', the World Wide Web can be seen as a 'network of documents'.

It is also crucial to understand that Internet without the World Wide Web was very impractical.

Indeed, it was theoretically possible for anybody connected to the Internet to communicate with other individuals, but in practice it was very difficult: each system had a diverse language. Therefore, for two persons to talk, the precondition was that both systems had the capability to speak the same language, which was hardly ever the case. For this reasons, the Internet was far from universal: it was constricting.

---

[21] Wikipedia's definition. http://en.wikipedia.org/wiki/World_Wide_Web

A solution was proposed in 1989 by Mr. Tim Berners-Lee[22] (today *Sir* Tim Berners-Lee[23]), a CERN (the European Organization for Nuclear Research) employee.

The system he conceived was one without a hierarchy: a "web" of information, connected through links, which main strength was that it had as few rules as possible so that everybody could use it. It would have been indeed nearly impossible to get everybody to use the same language or protocol to run their computer networks, as each local network has different local needs and preferences. It would have been the same thing as asking to a group of individuals, each one with a different nationality, to start a conversation in a language that was none's mother tongue. Thus Berners-Lee created what is commonly known as a 'markup language' - a modern system to add footnotes to a text in a way that is syntactically distinct (i.e. in another color or font) from that text. The idea and terminology comes from the "marking up" of manuscripts, in other words, the revision that editors operate on the manuscript that they receive from writers. Another simple example are the unspoken directions written on a movie screenplay to help the actors to place their voice and face expression.

Berners-Lee named his mark up language the 'Hyper Text Mark up Language' whose acronym is the very well known 'HTML'.

The creation of the World Wide Web made the Internet public. You no longer require a permission to share or announce something to the world. You no longer have to be a big private business, or a large institution; you no longer have to turn to a Television or Radio station or channel and ask for a license; you no longer have to pay newspapers to publish your ideas or thoughts. Gone are the barriers and the vast costs that one had to incur to access and to convey information. The lack of organizations exerting a certain type of control over the Internet remains as of today one of its main peculiarities as it enables its expansion at a yearly rate that exceeds 100% [24]. This was Sir Tim Berners-Lee's vision.

---

[22] Cailliau, R. & Gillies, J. (2000). *How the Web was born.* 1st Edition. New York. Oxford University Press Inc.

[23] Sir Tim Berners-Lee's is director of the World Wide Web Consortium (W3C) (http://www.w3.org/) founder of the World Wide Web Foundation; senior researcher and holder of the 3Com Founders Chair at the MIT Computer Science and Artificial Intelligence Laboratory (CSAIL); director of The Web Science Research Initiative (WSRI); member of the advisory board of the MIT Center for Collective Intelligence and member of the United States National Academy of Sciences, based in Washington, D.C.

[24] http://www.internetworldstats.com/stats.htm

Like a child hitting puberty, Internet has undergone a metamorphosis. We don't use it only to share documents anymore. We have websites, whose interfaces are now more colourful, pleasant to the eyes, easy to use. It is not just a question of 'looks', rather a question of 'what use do we make of it'.

Paragraph 2.3: The Web 2.0.

The old Internet was indeed a web of 'static' websites, whose changes were all dictated by their creators. It connected computers and made information available but that was mainly it. Today, with the web, not only computers (and therefore individuals) are connected but we are also witnessing new kinds of collaboration: information is not simply transferred from one computer to another, it is placed on websites were hundred of thousands of individuals can consult it. Moreover, content is not only shared, it is also created on these online websites.

That is how the term Web 2.0 was born: to describe this evolution of the Internet and of the World Wide Web, from a series of static sites connected among them, to a global environment in which online softwares, broadband connections and multimedia applications are able to offer wider contents and tighter connection among users than before. This is the first reason for which we have a 2.0 next to it, because it is seen as 'the second version' of the World Wide Web – like a software update. In other words, we could talk about the 'web 1.0' when referring to the World Wide Web created by Sir Berners-Lee and the 'web 2.0' when referring to all the web applications that have emerged in the last ten years and that were crucial for the manifestation of social media.

The other reason is that this new 'web' is bi-directional. Put in another way, the flow of information follows *two* paths. We have just explained again the use of the symbol 2.0: indeed information is not conveyed only in one direction, from the website to the user, but also from the user to the website. Today users are active participators and creators of what can be found on the Internet. This led, for instance, to the creation of terms such as 'user generated content" (UGC) [25]. The most mentioned example of such participative behaviour is the famous free online encyclopaedia 'Wikipedia'. In one sentence, we are talking about "applications that get better the more people use them", as answered by Mr. O'Reilly when interviewed by The Economist weekly newsmagazine in March 2010 [26].

The problem is that the person who invented the World Wide Web, and the one that thought up the term Web 2.0 do not agree on this reasoning. The latter presents the Web 2.0 as a new and improved version of the first Web, a version that would not be here if I hadn't been for his work and that of his company. The former agues that the Web 2.0 is simply the natural evolution of the World Wide Web, which was all about 'connecting people' right from the beginning. In his opinion the phrase 'web 2.0' is just a 'piece of jargon' [27], as he explicitly projected the Web to embody these values in the first place.

Who are we talking about? Dale Dougherty and Sir Tim Berners-Lee.

Dale Dougherty[28], vice president of O'Reilly Media, coined this new term and made it official during the first Web 2.0 conference, promoted in 2004 [29] by the same O'Reilly Media [30].

According to him Web 2.0 refers to an attitude towards the collaboration and the sharing of contents, enabled by software systems developed to support web interactions. This evolutionary approach is based upon the use of Web 2.0 as a platform.

However, neither Dale Dougherty nor Tim O'Reilly [31] (head of the O'Reilly Media) have worded an accurate definition of the Web 2.0. Without beating around the bush,

---

[25] Wunsch-Vincent, S. & Vickery. G. (2007). Participative Web: User-Created Content. Report prepared as as part of the WPIE work on Digital Content. Published on the responsibility of the Secretary-General of the OECD http://www.oecd.org/dataoecd/57/14/38393115.pdf.

[26] O'Reilly, T. (2010). *Six Years in The Valley*. Interviewed by The Economist during the economist 'Innovation Event' held in Berkeley. Audio format found at:
http://video.economist.com/index.jsp?fr_story=7c533c16196b81c7fb025dde3688dfd34626dda0.

[27] Laningham, S. (2006). *DeveloperWorks Interviews: Tim Berners-Lee*. Blogpost/Interview.
http://www.ibm.com/developerworks/podcast/dwi/cm-int082206txt.html.

[28] Dale Dougherty: http://www.oreillynet.com/pub/au/26

[29] Di Bari, V. (2007). *Web 2.0 : Internet è cambiato. E voi? : i consigli dei principali esperti italiani e internazionali per affrontare le nuove sfide.* 1st Edition. Milan. Il Sole 24 Ore.

[30] O'Reilly, T. (2005). *What is Web 2.0*. Blogpost. http://oreilly.com/web2/archive/what-is-web-20.html.

[31] O'Reilly, T. & Musser, J. (2006). *Web 2.0: principles and best practices.* 1st Edition. USA. O'Reilly Media.

Web 2.0 is simply the denomination that got the most successful, thanks to O'Reilly Media's astute and wise marketing and promotional activities. In this scenario, the absence of a unique definition contributed to increase the international debate, which is still going on, and the interest about the term Web 2.0.

This is the problem: there still is a lot of divergence surrounding the term Web 2.0 and want it means, with some people denouncing it as a "*meaningless marketing buzzword*" [32], and others acknowledging it as the new conventional knowledge.

In O'Reilly's opinion, the fact that the term Web 2.0 has become popular must mean that it is "*as good a term as any*" and that we may see this querelle as the "*old debate between language purists and language pragmatists*" [33] i.e. that it all depends on whether you think that the right words are the ones people actually use or not. What cannot be denied is that Web 2.0 has become popular.

Moreover, it looks like the two Tims have sort of made up[34].

But which Web 2.0's features in particular were crucial for Social Media's manifestation?

The first is undoubtedly **content sharing** (enabled by interconnection).

At the very beginning, it was possible to share information from one computer to another (*one-to-one*). This meant that maximum two persons were benefiting from it – this was for instance the main degree of sharing within the Arpanet and then later with the first e-mail softwares.

The second information-sharing pattern is *one-to-many*. Take as an example the first websites that appeared on the net: there the information was conveyed by one entity, often a private firm or a big public institution trying either to advertise and increase its brand image and awareness or to inform its clients and employees by making certain information publicly available on the internet. We are the 'many' in this phrase.

Then came the third degree of information sharing, *many-to-many*. It started with *forums* populating the web and continues now in particular with Wikis[35].

---

[32] O'Reilly, T. (2005). *What is Web 2.0*. Blogpost. http://oreilly.com/web2/archive/what-is-web-20.html.

[33] O'Reilly, T. (2005). *Not 2.0?* Blogpost. http://radar.oreilly.com/2005/08/not-20.html

[34] Sir Tim Berners-Lee interviewed by Tim O'Reilly during the last *Web 2.0 Summit* (2009). Video http://www.youtube.com/watch?v=KY5skobffk0&feature=player_embedded. San Francisco.

[35] Wikis. Originally the Haitian word for 'fast' (*wiki wiki*), a wiki is a collective Web page that allows users to post or link content without having to use HTML. The most known example is the free online encyclopedia Wikipedia (www.wikipedia.com). Other examples are: Wikianswers, wikiquotes, wikitravels, etc.

The fourth and last degree to which information can be shared is said *many-to-one*. It means that the information (the inputs) provided by a multitude of users is aggregated and reunited into a single voice.

If we define an online practice a 'Social Media' it means that it allows content sharing at all the four levels simultaneously.

Social Media are hence the web applications that enable this **interoperability**. The crucial characteristic of social media is how they place users at the centre of everything, as they are the ones consuming and producing the content displayed through them. As evidence, take TIME's cover on December 13, 2006 [36] (Figure 1.1):

Figure 1.1 Time's cover on December 13, 2006.

Social Media have enabled individuals to produce and create content (of any type) at a considerable speed. We are witnessing a true explosion of creativity. In the Fashion and Luxury sector, for instance, Fast Fashion retailers such as H&M or Mass brands like American Apparel are running *online photographic contest*. The luxury

---

[36] Grossman, L. (2006). *Time's person of the Year: You.* Newspaper' article. Time Publications. USA. http://www.time.com/time/magazine/article/0,9171,1569514,00.html

"Who are these people? Seriously, who actually sits down after a long day at work and says, I'm not going to watch Lost tonight. I'm going to turn on my computer and make a movie starring my pet iguana? I'm going to mash up 50 Cent's vocals with Queen's instrumentals? I'm going to blog about my state of mind or the state of the nation or the steak-frites at the new bistro down the street? Who has that time and that energy and that passion?

The answer is, you do. And for seizing the reins of the global media, for founding and framing the new digital democracy, for working for nothing and beating the pros at their own game, TIME's Person of the Year for 2006 is you."

brand Bulgari is promoting the launch of a new jewels' line by organizing an event exclusively addressed to *fashion bloggers*. Louis Vuitton has a *Facebook group* through which its fans can watch the *broadcasted catwalk show live* on the Internet. Fashion designers and executives are constantly sharing their thoughts with the whole world by *twitting* at least once a day.

Paragraph 2.4: The Social Media Ecosystem – background basics of each tool.

As you may have noticed, there is quite a *lot* of vocabulary in the paragraph up here that does not appear (yet) in your dictionary. As a conclusion to this second chapter, let us define quickly the main Social Media tools:

- **Social Networks–FaceBook, Twitter, LinkedIn** [37].

When Social Media started connecting with each other, creating thereby an interconnected group, exchanging information and contents, they gave birth to Social Networks – in the very same way the interconnected computers gave birth in 1987 to the most famous network ever – Internet.
Here is a list of the most known and used Social Networks:

Facebook [38] – Created in 2004 by Mark Zuckerberg (along with Dustin Moskovitz, Eduardo Saverin, and Chris Hughes) while attending Harvard University.
Zuckerberg & co.'s initial idea was that of creating a social network offering to its users the benefits of the traditional student book published at the end of every academic year in basically any American college, a book where each student, faculty or staff member had a personal page complete with headshot photos, dedications received and contacts - a book renowned as the "Facebook."
The online Facebook begun just as a "Harvard-thing," meaning that only Harvard students could register to and use it. Only subsequently it spread to other schools like Stanford, Dartmouth, New York University, or Yale (for instance), then to

---

[37] Riva, G. (2010). *Che cos'e' un social network: la fusione tra reti reali e reti virtuali*. Power point presentation. http://www.scribd.com/doc/27103243/Che-cos-e-un-Social-Network.
[38] Pearlman, L. & Abram, C. (2010). *Facebook® for Dummies® 2nd Edition*. Hoboken. Wiley Publishing Inc.

organizations and companies within the U.S, to English-speaking countries in 2004 and became finally global in 2006.

Today Facebook is the most known and used social network worldwide, with more than 500 millions users as of July 2010 [39]. What made Facebook so popular are its friendly to use interfaces, the option to join a thousand different groups, to keep in touch with friends and colleagues by posting on their 'walls', by 'adding' them to our own private network of friends or by sending them messages. Finally, the possibility to share and post basically any type of content format (blogposts, music, videos and photos) was also a major attraction. Facebook main strength is indeed the fact that it works as an open source platform[40].

LinkedIn [41] – a social networking site for business professionals, decisions makers and influencers who want to be 'linked in' (i.e. linked up, forming a connection with) and whose average age is 43 years old. Created in 2003 by Reid Hoffman, it is mainly used to conduce professional and job-related networking. LinkedIn surpassed 50 millions users in October 2009 [42]. This is the right network for who needs to promote him/herself on the job arena and to self-advertise to specific business audiences. Indeed, the difference with Facebook, for example, is that LinkedIn researches and finds not only individuals but also companies. Some advantages of using LinkedIn are: being introduced to new potential customers, finding business partners and suppliers and introducing people to each other. The latter in particular is LinkedIn main upside: since the network works through degrees (three, to be precise) the number of individuals you can actually contact in a matter of minutes is actually much higher than the number of your real connections. For instance, if your connections – your trusted friends and colleagues – are 100, and each of them has another 100 connections, this means that 'at two degrees away' you can reach 10.000 individuals. If the 100 friends of your friends also have 100 connections at the first degree then 'at three degrees away' (in this network) you can reach a maximum of 1 million individuals and pass them your introduction.

[39] Zuckerberg, M. (2010). *500 Million Stories*. Blog Post
http://blog.facebook.com/blog.php?post=409753352130.
[40] Pavone, L. (2010). *Social Media e Editoria Online: relazione virtuosa o pericolosa?* Power Point presentation. IAB seminar.
[41] Elad, J. (2008). *LinkedIn® For Dummies®*. Hoboken. Wiley Publishing Inc.
[42] Warren, C. (2009). LinkedIn surpasses 50 millions users. Blogpost.
http://mashable.com/2009/10/14/linkedin-50-millon/.

Twitter [43]– a 'microblogging' website that enables users to send messages made up of 140 characters or less – relabeled 'tweets'[44]. As of June 2010, Twitter's COO Dick Costolo tweeted that Twitter has more than 190 millions users [45]; however Barracuda Labs' 2009 annual report [46] states that only 21% of Twitter users are *really using* twitter, and can hence be defined as 'True Twitter Users'. The conditions to be described as a true twitter user are the following: you must have at least 10 followers, you must follow at least 10 people and you must have tweeted at least 10 times. This means that Twitter's real users are 'only' 39,9 millions.

Table 1.1 – Social Networks' Comparison.

Social Network	Facebook	Twitter	LinkedIn
Date of Birth	2004	2006	2003
Creator	Mark Zuckerberg	Jack Dorsey	Reid Hoffman
Networking through the use of:	'wall posts' and 'private messages'	'tweets'	Connections, participation to forums
Network made of	'Friends'	'Followers'	'your connections', 'two degrees' and 'three degrees'
Possibility to post:	Videos, photos, music, notes,	No posting, only re-twitting or linking pre-existent content	A replica of the Curriculum Vitae
Degree of Privacy	Customizable	Has to be inexistent to engender any kind of benefits	Customizable

---

[43] Fitton, L., Gruen, M. & Poston, L. (2010). *Twitter® For Dummies® 2nd Edition*. Hoboken. Wiley Publishing Inc.
[44] This is why it is defined as 'microblogging website'. A 'tweet' is the chirp of a small bird, a short and sharp sound. This is precisely what the creator of Twitter, Jack Dorsey had in mind when he invented twitter: having a social network/platform on which people could interact only through 'short and sharp' remarks and comments – the tweets!
[45] Costolo, D. (2010). Tweet post. http://twitter.com/exectweets/status/15705793585.
[46] Barracuda Labs' Annual Report 2009. PDF Format.
http://barracudalabs.com/downloads/BarracudaLabs2009AnnualReport-FINAL.pdf

- **Visual Sharing – Flickr (Photos) and YouTube (Videos)**

Flickr is an image and video hosting website with its very own online community that shares and comments on posted visual contents. Founded and launched in 2004 by the Ludicorp Company [47] and acquired one year later by Yahoo, Flickr is widely used by Twitters and Bloggers to post photos taken with their mobile phone (or any other portable device equipped with both an internet connection and a camera) directly to their blog, Facebook profile or Twitter profile from their Flickr account [48].

YouTube [49] is a video sharing website where users can view, share and upload videos. Created in February 2005 by Steve Chen, Chad Hurley and Jawed Karim, YouTube was bought in 2006 by Google. Amateur videos (another way to describe user-generated videos) are YouTube's main content. Individuals shoot, post produce and upload them on their own. YouTube is one of the best examples of Web 2.0 technologies.

It should be noted that Social Media have become over the last decade a permanent tool for a company's media plan, particularly because of their market coverage and penetration. For instance, an article published by The Nielsen Company on their blog 'Nielsenwire' on June 15, 2010[50] regarding a research conducted in Brazil, France, Italy, Switzerland, US, UK, Spain, Germany and Australia, demonstrates how the coupled 'consumption' (the average time spent) on YouTube, Wikipedia and Facebook accounts for 22 percent of all time online. This means that, for every four minutes spent online by an average visitor of the Internet, one is dedicated exclusively to the use of Social Networks and/or Blogs. The average time spent on Facebook worldwide in April 2010 was, for example, of 6 hours per month (according to this ranking, Facebook is indeed out of the three, the most popular one), nearly 1 hour per month for YouTube and 15 minutes for Wikipedia, as seen in Table 1.2.

[47] Ludicorp official website: www.ludicorp.com
[48] Terdiman, D. (2004). *Photo Site a Hit With Bloggers*. Blogpost.
http://www.wired.com/culture/lifestyle/news/2004/12/65958. Wired.
[49] Sahlin, D. & Botello, C. (2007). *YouTube™ for Dummies®*. Hoboken. Wiley Publishing.
[50] *Social Networks/Blogs Now Account for One in Every Four and a Half Minutes Online*
http://blog.nielsen.com/nielsenwire/global/social-media-accounts-for-22-percent-of-time-online/

Table 1.2

WORLD'S* MOST POPULAR BRANDS ONLINE / April 2010		
Brand	% of World's Internet Population visiting brand	Time per person (hh:mm:ss)
Google	82%	1:21:51
MSN/WindowsLive/Bing	62%	2:41:49
Facebook	54%	6:00:00
Yahoo!	53%	1:50:16
Microsoft	48%	0:45:31
YouTube	47%	0:57:33
Wikipedia	35%	0:13:26
AOL Media Network	27%	2:01:02
eBay	26%	1:34:08
Apple	26%	1:00:28
Source: The Nielsen Company *Global refers to AU, BR, CH, DE, ES, FR, IT, UK & USA only		

- **Publishing: Blogs and Vlogs**

Blog is short for "Web log"[51]. Hence, just as a 'log' is a regular or systematic record of observations or an official record of events during a journey, a 'web log' is a web journal, an 'online diary' where the 'owner', the one creating the content, can post what excites him the most and share it with whoever surfs the web. When creating a

---

[51] The term 'weblog' was coined for the first time the 17th of december 1997 by blogger Jorn Barger. http://www.wired.com/culture/lifestyle/news/2007/12/blog_advice.
The term 'blog' was instead coined by Peter Merholz in 1999.
McCullagh, D. & Broache, A. (2007). *Blogs turn 10--who's the father? Blogging has been around for about a decade now--depending on how you define it and whom you ask.* CNET News.com, (c) CNET Networks Inc.USA.

blog, users can fill it with whatever they want: comments, news, photos, videos, etc. Often, they also let readers post feedback, creating thereby an exchange of ideas by written words. Fashion Blogs (see Paragraph 3.1) are just one of the many kinds of different blogs that we can find online. Bloglovin[52], the online platform where subscribers can create they very own list of blogs to follow, has over 8455 blogs registered under the term 'fashion blogs'.

Vlogs are 'video blogs', i.e. online journals where the 'owner' communicates with and updates its 'followers' through videos instead of written blogposts. Fashion vlogs are very rare given the fact that they would have to be fashion blogs where the majority of posts are videos. Fashion blogs can be at maximum considered 'photo blogs': nearly all posts have indeed at least one picture attached to it, while videos are generally posted only when the blogger gets the chance – for instance – to go backstage at a fashion show or he/she is invited in the showroom of a certain brand, to get a preview of the next collection, and he/she wants to share this experience with her/his readers.

- **Audio Sharing**

The clearest example of what can be defined as an audio sharing social media is the 'podcast': an audio file distributed over the Internet through Really Simple Syndication (RSS - a technology that lets users subscribe to feeds that deliver wiki or blog updates or even more general information such as another syndication feed).
Podcast first appeared on the iPod – the origin of the term. A fashion podcast could be, for example, an interview to a certain designer or fashion manager although they are quite rare, since fashion and luxury tend to compete mostly in the symbolic arena, where images have a large predominance over words. Hence, if an interview to a fashion key spokesperson is to be delivered, it will probably be under the form of a video interview.

- **Virtual Worlds & Gaming**

Virtual worlds are simply online worlds, parallel to our real life in the flesh. The most known virtual reality is SecondLife, born as a virtual place where anyone can give

---

[52] http://www.bloglovin.com/search/fashion+blog

free rein to one's imagination – within certain limits – through a personal 'avatar', the movable icon representing a person in this cyberspace. Some fashion companies, such as Giorgio Armani, built quite a fortune thanks to SecondLife by selling their virtual products for real money. Virtual worlds are not however a recent and, most importantly, growing phenomenon. Hence, we will not address them further in this thesis.

- **Mobile**

One characteristic that certainly contributed to the success of Social Media is that they all also come as 'mobile applications': Twitter in particular is, in the majority of cases, accessed through portable devices, such as mobile phones or smart phones accessorized with a photo camera. The invention of the iPhone and of the iPad[53] has certainly contributed to improve the accessibility to the Internet whenever and wherever.

I hope to have provided with this chapter a simple, linear and clear, yet comprehensive, definition of Social Media.

Let's now turn our attention to the qualitative data gathered for this thesis.

---

[53] (2010). The Connected Devices Age: iPads, Kindles, Smartphones and the Connected Consumer. http://blog.nielsen.com/nielsenwire/consumer/the-connected-devices-age-ipads-kindles-smartphones-and-the-connected-consumer/

Chapter Three: Cases Description.

To test whether Social Media are the new essential tool to be paired with Old media – or not – I report here as empirical evidence some examples of Fashion and Luxury companies that have indeed used these latter within their communication strategy, as well as some instances of exclusively fashion related social media. The latter open this third chapter. The cases presented here have been chosen according to the amount of reliable information available and to the magnitude of the buzz they have created. Social Media Coverage was measured when possible with Google's 'Doubleclick Add Planner application'[54]. Unfortunately, Facebook pages and Twitter accounts are incompatible with this application. Therefore, to estimate the number of people that visit and visualize these websites we relied on the number of 'followers' of each Twitter account and on the number of 'likes' for each Facebook page.

Paragraph 3.1: Social Media Tools that are exclusively fashion-related.

- **Lookbook**

LOOKBOOK.nu (LB) is a community website founded at the end of 2007/beginning 2008[55] as an online archive for street styles and is owned by Spacedock inc., a California corporation. The community describes itself as an *"international social experiment in style [...] inspired by street fashion blogs like 'The Sartorialist*[56]*"*. Hence, users log on LB (prior to March 2010 an invitation from a member was required; since then anyone can join) and 'post' an outfit of their choice (following certain posting rules[57]) in the hope of being recognized by the community as possessing a certain 'style' or 'fashion sense'. Members' appraisal is manifested through 'hypes' that are engendered by clicking on the photo one likes. The more hypes one gets, the more his or her looks will be seen by a larger number of people,

---

[54] https://www.google.com/adplanner. All data retrieved thanks to Google's doubleclick add planner application and presented in this thesis refers to a specific period of time, i.e. September 2010.
[55] December 27, 2007 is the date reported on the following website http://www.outerstats.com/site/lookbook.nu. However the copyright found on the lookbook official website, bearing the name of the owning company spacedock Inc. indicates year 2008.
[56] www.thesartorialist.com
[57] http://forum.lookbook.nu/help

the more he or she will be able to get value and fame within the community (this is the maximal aspiration for anyone joining lookbook).

What started off as an experiment is today a consolidated and sort of recognized authority for what concerns fashion related Internet websites. In July 2010, lookbook.nu was visited by 610 thousands new unique visitors[58] (the estimated and unduplicated number of people who visit a site, according to Google's doubleclick ad planner application). Lookbook.nu also has a Twitter account[59], 'followed' by 57,844 individuals and a Facebook account[60] 'liked' by 269,308 (as off November 1, 2010). These numbers keep growing at a remarkable pace on September 27, Lookbook's twitter followers were 55,548, whiles its Facebook 'likes' amounted to 222,935.

- **Fashion Blogs**

In the first part of this thesis we explained what a blog is: a web journal, an 'online diary' where the 'owner', the one creating the content (the blogger), can post what excites him the most (enhancing the description with photos, videos, links or reported discussions) and share it with whoever surfs the web. With the active participation of readers, blogs often become an active exchange of written ideas.

Fashion Blogs in particular are those blogs covering subject regarding the fashion industry, by reporting, for instance, a fashion show or an interview to a fashion insider, its offering (talking about a new collection or a certain fashion item, whether it is an accessory or a piece of clothing) and style (street or personal, new trends, what celebrities wear, etc.).

Some fashion blogs are regarded as being mainly shopping advice websites. This phenomenon is however more limited to beauty and skin care related blogs.

No one really knows when exactly did the first fashion blog appear, just as nobody can not really agree on who created the first blog[61]. What is certain, is that blogs exist since as early as 1997, and that the first fashion blog entirely dedicated to

---

[58]https://www.google.com/adplanner/planning/site_profile#siteDetails?identifier=Lookbook.nu&lp=true

[59] http://twitter.com/lookbookdotnu

[60] http://www.facebook.com/LOOKBOOK.nu

[61] McCullagh, D. & Broache, A. (2007). *Blogs turn 10--who's the father? Blogging has been around for about a decade now--depending on how you define it and whom you ask.* CNET News.com, (c) CNET Networks Inc.USA.

shoes and women accessory (for instance) was created in 2004[62]. Hence, in 2007, US print media were already definitively very interested in fashion blogs[63].

The main characteristic of a blog is that all the information reported in it is biased by the blogger point of view. Bloggers are not indeed journalists. Hence, two fashion blogs may report the same exact content and still produce two very diverse outcomes. The determinant factor is the author's writing style and personality. The success of the blog often depends solely on the latter.
This is at least how fashion blogging started.

While today the blogosphere is full of fashion blogs put into practice by Fashion and Luxury companies themselves (fashion and luxury's companies' official blogs are not the same as their official website; on the contrary, their layout resembles very much – and inspiration was clearly taken – form consumers' fashion blogs. e.g. Chanel http://chanel-news.chanel.com/en/, Costume National http://blog.cnc-costumenational.com/, Max Mara http://blog.maxmara.com/en/, and Dolce and Gabbana http://www.swide.com/luxury-magazine) so as to create a direct contact with end consumers, the very first fashion blogs were the online diaries (mainly) of outsiders, i.e. individuals *not* working in the fashion industry, some of whom very smart and very, very young (like Tavi Gevinson from http://www.thestylerookie.com/) with an undeniable passion about fashion, who were discussing and following it with professionalism and competence.

Other fashion blogs, such as www.thesartorialist.com by Mr. Scott Schuman, or www.garancedore.fr by Ms Garance Doré, with 100.000 new unique visitors each per month[64], started off, and still are, more about the pictures and less about texts and comments – the latter are indeed best defined as street style blogs or photo blogs.

---

[62] http://shoeblogs.com/2006/12/05/manolo-the-first-fashion-blogger/
[63] http://www.dailymail.co.uk/femail/article-428821/The-fashion-blog-stars.html

[64] Google doubleclick ad planner resuls for the sartorialist
https://www.google.com/adplanner/planning/site_profile#siteDetails?identifier=www.thesartorialist.com&lp=true
Google doubleclick ad planner resuls for garancedore.fr
https://www.google.com/adplanner/planning/site_profile#siteDetails?identifier=garancedore.fr&geo=001&trait_type=1&lp=true

The number of visits, i.e. of individuals that read these blogs each month, for the first time, is impressive. Vogue Italia, for instance, has 'only' 66.476 readers per month[65]. But what all fashion bloggers had in common as a start was that none, or at least a very little number of them, had any of the fashion press' obligations. They were welcomed as a breath of fresh air in an industry where the relationship between creators and reporters had perhaps become too tight and needy. Compared to the traditional means of mass communication, they had the advantage of being independent from any possible scheme, even if they certainly lacked the experience that can only be built after years and years of 'being there'.

Notwithstanding the fact that many had defined fashion blogging as a temporary phenomenon, in 2008 and 2009, it started to spread in Italy as well. Some fashion journalists had unquestionably felt threatened[66] by this new sudden army of wannabes. In the USA, some bloggers had indeed started collaborations with fashion magazines, brands and stylists, hence becoming part of the mainstream fashion press.

This is when things started to change. While the first fashion bloggers had undeniably started a blog out of inspiration, the most recently opened fashion blogs are increasingly created by individuals that are clearly 'fashion aspiring insiders'[67], i.e. individuals who have a strong desire to work in the fashion industry or within the fashion media arena and therefore use their blog as a back or side entrance. Some even do it merely in the hope of being invited to a fashion show.

In addition, more and more people are opening fashion blogs mainly – if not exclusively- because the latter have become highly profitable. Bloggers can earn money by selling advertising to some brands (fast fashion retailers H&M and American Apparel have indeed bought advertising on fashion blogs). This monetization technique is called 'pay per click': the blogger is paid by the advertiser –

---

[65] Data provided by Prima Comunicazione (http://www.primaonline.it/2010/09/09/83187/diffusione-dei-mensili-maggio-2010/). The data has been dilvuged by editors who also autorized the publication. The data refers to the moving average/rolling mean over the period lasting from June 2009 to May 2010. 66.476 is the number of copies sold (half of which come from subscription), not of copies *divulged*, as there is no guarantee that the later may have been read by someone.

[66] Wilson, E. (2009). *Bloggers Crash Fashion's Front Row.* Newspapers' article. The New York Times.
[67] Corcoran, C. T. (2006). *Blogging for bags - A growing group of writers is chatting up accessories.* Women's Wear Daily. Copyright 2006 Fairchild Publications, Inc.

in this case H&M – each time an H&M advertising on his/her blog is clicked by a visitor[68].

There is nothing wrong if what started out as a hobby acquires some monetary value and hence becomes a source of financial sustainability and reward, especially if the latter requires hard work.

But isn't it a different matter if one starts a fashion blog exclusively for monetary reasons?

We will further discuss this in the Fourth Chapter, when addressing factors that could lead to an unsuccessful use of Social Media within the Fashion and Luxury Industry.

- **Fashion Vlogs**

Vlogs are blogs where the content is mainly conveyed through videos. The videos that appear in fashion blogs do not however represent a sufficient percentage over the total number of posts issued by the blog for the blog to be classified as a vlog. Within fashion blogs videos are indeed often used as complement of a post, the text and pictures remaining the central focus. Examples of videos uploaded on fashion blogs are, for instance, videos of a catwalk show, behind the scenes reportages, interviews to fashion insiders, videos showing the latest trends or the new season trends. This is the case if the videos are created and uploaded by the blogger him/herself. Otherwise, videos within a fashion blog are mainly 'video links': the blogger copies the link of a video presentation of a company's new product and simply posts it on the blog.

Fashion vlogs are hence very rare, if nonexistent, and this is why we will not further discuss them here.

---

[68] Google's doubleclick ad planner applications among other information also tells if a certain website accepts advertising.

Paragraph 3.2: Events promoted through social media

- ### The case of the Metropolitan Mass Fashion brand: H&M.

'H & M Hennes & Mauritz AB' is a Swedish fashion group founded in 1947 by Erling Persson (if truth be told, the first store opened in 1947 in Västerås was called simply Hennes. It changed to Hennes and Mauritz only in 1968). It operates in the sector of apparel and fashion accessories for men, women (for which also a cosmetic line was started in 1977), teenagers and children and has become worldwide famous for the brand that bears the same name. Other brands owned by the group[69] are COS[70], Monki[71], Weekday[72] and Cheap Monday[73]. Its business concept rotates around the idea of providing "*fashion and quality at the best price*".

Some important dates and facts in H&M's growth process: in the 1990s it was one of the first fast fashion retailers brands to use famous models in its advertising campaigns; in 1998 it started Internet sales; in 2004 was celebrated the first (with Karl Lagerfeld) of the many to come designer collaborations (further collaborations include Stella McCartney, Viktor & Rolf, Roberto Cavalli, Sonia Rykiel[74], Matthew Williamson, Jimmy Choo, Comme des Garçons[75]) and from 2006 onwards there has been an expansion of Internet and catalogues sales.

Today H&M has 2,066 stores (as of July 31st, 2010[76]) in 35 different markets and around 76,000 employees. Sales in 2009 reached 119 billion Sweden kronor[77] (SEK) which corresponds to approximately 12.7 billion euros or 16.1 billion dollars[78] and

---

[69] http://www.hm.com/gb/investorrelations/hmandourotherbrands__multibrand.nhtml
[70] COS Offical Website: http://www.cosstores.com/gb/site/about__about.nhtml
[71] http://monkiworld.com/
[72] http://www.weekday.se/
[73] http://www.cheapmonday.com/about
[74] http://www.hm.com/gb/press/pressreleases/__prfashion.nhtml?pressreleaseid=942
[75] http://www.hm.com/gb/press/pressreleases/__prfashion.nhtml?pressreleaseid=681
[76] H&M Group sales development in July:
http://www.hm.com/gb/press/financialreports/salesdevelopment/financepressrelease.ahtml?pressreleas eid=506793&nodeid=1,028
[77] http://www.hm.com/gb/press/financialreports/annualreports__pressinvestorannualreports.nhtml
[78] These conversions were calculated using live rates at 2010-08-30, the conversion rate for Sweden Kronors to Euros being 0.106481 and that for SEK to USD being 0.135495. Soure: Universal Currency Converter™ http://www.xe.com/ucc/convert.cgi?Amount=119&From=SEK&To=EUR

thanks to good cost control (and despite the economic downturn on sales), profit for the same year reached SEK 16.4 billion[79] ($\approx$ EUR 1.75 billion or USD 2.3 billion)."

As stated in the previous chapter, lookbook.nu was visited, in July 2010, by 610 thousands new unique visitors. This considerable traffic of data and affluence of fashion-concerned users on a unique website did not go unnoticed by companies that were already using Internet as a communication channel. H&M, as mentioned up here, was one of them.

The 1st of February 2010 'The Blues' contest sponsored by H&M was launched on the lookbook.nu website. Community members were asked to 'post' a 'look' that would respect lookbook.nu standard posting rules but with at least one H&M item (to be specified or 'tagged' in the caption) and at least two items of the color blue. The prize to win: among the most hyped looks, H&M editors would choose 35, and publish them five by five, each week, on H&M's official website. Each one the 35 winners received a €100.00 gift certificate to be spent in any H&M store. When the contest ended, on March 19th, 1544 pictures had been submitted.

This is not the only use of fashion-related social media by H&M: the brand also invited some of the most known 'fashion bloggers' to its Cheap Monday catwalk show on the 21st of August during Stockholm's last fashion week. The guest bloggers reported their impressions on their blogs, with comments, pictures and videos[80]. Moreover, H&M dedicated part of its official website (www.hm.com which registered 4.6 millions unique visitors in August 2010 [81]) to social media.

This area of the website is called 'the social media room' (http://www.hm.com/gb/socialmediaroom socialMediaRoom.nhtml): it perfectly integrates any Social Network or Social Media in which H&M appears or is mentioned, like Twitter[82], where H&M is 'followed' by 63,884 individuals and Facebook[83], where 4,705,240 people (as off November 1, 2010[84]) have 'liked' (subscribed to) the page.

---

[79] H & M HENNES & MAURITZ AB Full-Year Report
http://www.hm.com/gb/press/financialreports/interimreports/financepressrelease.ahtml?pressreleaseid=469095&nodeid=1,027
[80] http://www.stylescrapbook.com/2010/08/cheap-monday.html
[81] Google's doubleclick add planner results for H&M's official website
https://www.google.com/adplanner/planning/site_profile#siteDetails?identifier=hm.com&lp=true
[82] http://twitter.com/hm/
[83] http://www.facebook.com/hm

Figure 3.1 – contest rules appearing on lookbook.nu

Figure 3.2 – the first five winners of the contest. The first three are reknowed fashion bloggers: Bryanboy (http://bryanboy.com), Andreas Wijk (http://kanal5.se/andreaswijk) and Denni Ellas (http://thechicmuse.blogspot.com/).

- **The case of the Avant-Garde Mass Fashion Brand: American Apparel.**

Another brand that collaborated with Lookbook in a similar way to H&M is American Apparel.

American Apparel® is an American vertically integrated[85] manufacturer (American apparel factory is actually the largest garment factory within the US, as the majority has moved abroad to enjoy cheaper labor), distributor and retailer (since 2003), founded in 1989 by Canadian Dov Charney and based from year 2000 in downtown Los Angeles, California. The company is publicly listed on the American stock

---

[84] On September 27, 2010 the likes were 3,758,145 and the followers 55,503. This gives an idea of Social Media exponential growth.

[85] Since the company is vertically integrated it does not rely on subcontractors nor foreign labor.

exchange. The brand is mostly known for the two main products categories with which it debuted two decades ago, T-shirts and underwear garments. During the years the offering expanded to similar and core related product categories such as leggings, top tanks, leotards, pants and dresses made of stretch fabric, jumpers, bathing suit, nail polishes[86] and accessories for women, men and children.

The company is expanding worldwide and plans to keep doing it: it is present in 19 different countries with 260 stores[87] and employs more than 10,000 workers[88].

Their official fact sheet reported 2009 net sales amounting to $558.8 million[89]; these numbers have however being questioned and considered as unreliable[90].

American Apparel is indeed a controversial company: on one hand it strives for value-oriented consumption (its products have no logo and they are produced in socially responsible settings); on the other, it is heavily criticized for its provocative advertising. These latter in particular have often caused quite a stir in consumers' associations[91].

These criticisms did not stop the collaboration between lookbook.nu and American Apparel. The 5th of December 2009 the 'How do you wear American Apparel?' contest was launched on the fashion community website. This was actually the very first contest of this type to be launched, as it preceded the H&M's 'The Blues'. The rules are again the same: each participant had to upload an outfit with at least one AA clothing garment. Sixteen days later, on New Year's Eve, the contest closed with 583 entries. The three winners chose by AA staff were invited to American Apparel headquarters in Downtown Los Angeles to be photographed in their own American Apparel ad campaign, while the 25 most hyped looks won a 25% off discount code redeemable at americanapparel.com[92].

Moreover, all the looks that participated to the contest were eligible to be included – and hence appear – in a special American Apparel catalogue: a 64-pages collection of 132 inspirational American Apparel looks created by 77 lookbook members,

---

[86] http://www.americanapparel.net/presscenter/articles/20091217wwd.html
[87] http://www.americanapparel.net/contact/2009_Fact_Sheet.pdf
[88] http://www.americanapparel.net/contact/profile.html
[89] http://investors.americanapparel.net/releasedetail.cfm?ReleaseID=454795
[90] http://www.observer.com/2010/daily-transom/american-apparel-sued-shareholders
[91] http://www.independent.co.uk/news/media/advertising/seminude-model-appeared-to-be-under-16-1780394.html
[92] http://lookbook.nu/contest/3-Win-An-American-Apparel-Modeling-Gig

chosen by AA editorial staff. The choice did not depend solely upon the number of 'hypes' received.

Once published, the booklet was distributed in AA stores around the world. It can still be purchased on the company official website[93].

Figure 3.3 – American Apparel contest on Lookbook.nu

Figure 3.4 – American Apparel x Lookbook Booklet.

[93] http://www.americanapparel.com/lookbook.html; http://lookbook.nu/log/135-THE-AA-X-LB-LOOKBOOK-HAS-LANDED- ; http://www.youtube.com/watch?v=EIYAiO-bqzk&feature=player_embedded

- **The case of the Classic Mass Fashion Brand: United Colors of Benetton.**

United Colors of Benetton (UCB) is the most known of the four mass fashion brands (the other three being Sisley, Undercolors of Benetton and Playlife) owned by the namesake publicly listed Italian Group founded in 1965.

UCB is a vertically integrated company operating in womenswear, menswear and childrenswear. It also recently expanded into home accessories, toiletries and perfumes.

A staff of 300 designers coming from all over the world creates the company offering.

UCB is present in more than 120 different countries with around 6,000 directly operated stores[94] (either of their property or given in franchise) situated in high traffic locations. Characterized by a colorful and casual style, UCB became internationally famous in the eighties, through its innovative advertising campaigns, directed by the renowned and controversial Italian photographer Oliviero Toscani. That was undeniably the company's peak moment and still is considered the period in which it gained the highest brand recognition.

Benetton was always considered 'avant-garde' for what concerns its communication strategy, particularly if compared with other mass fashion brands. The company has indeed its own communication research centre, Fabrica[95], created in 1994. Based in the Italian city of Treviso, Fabrica offers a one-year study grant to the most young artists and designers under 25 years old from all over the world, who find themselves in a privileged context characterized by a rich multicultural interchange and high opportunity for creative growth. In exchange, the young residents artists work on the brand's magazine 'Colors' and on the company's advertisings.

As Mr. Alessandro Benetton, executive deputy chairman of the Benetton Group and eldest son of founder Mr. Luciano Benetton puts it "Fabrica acts as a sort of telescope for us. [...] All the campaigns are the fruits of the ability of the people who work there, their responses to the specific requests of the company."[96].

The initiative "It's:My:Time" fits therefore perfectly with the company established brand image and identity.

---

[94] http://www.benettongroup.com/en/whoweare/stores.htm
[95] http://www.fabrica.it/
[96] Benetton, A. Interviewed by Burrows, T. (2010). Benetton's It's My Time: casting the net. Newspapers article. The Daily Telegraph. UK.
http://www.telegraph.co.uk/fashion/7482435/Benettons-Its-My-Time-casting-the-net.html

The 8th February 2010 the contest was launched through the company's advertisings, both with online (teaser video-clips on YouTube, Facebook and Mtv.com; Google banners; collaboration with independent fashion and communication related blogs) and print media (Augmented Reality ads and postcards with an AR code).

It regarded a global casting competition to 'discover new looks and new faces'. Whoever desired to participate, simply had to create an online 'look-book' by uploading photos and videos expressing his or her own style and personality on the following website: casting.benetton.com – the only rule being that participants must be at least 14 years old and have no existing modeling contracts[97].

The more votes were received by a candidate from other users, the higher the probability for him or her to be one of the 100 most voted contestants and hence be entitled to receive a €200.00 voucher by Benetton and to be featured in a book about global style.

In six weeks (from the 8th of February to the 16th of March), 65,085[98] individuals from 217 different countries participated to the event by uploading photos, videos or texts on the website. The latter received 3.9 millions unique visits. An absurd amount of traffic in such a short period of time.

As mentioned, Benetton's official casting website was not the only online tool used by the company to promote the initiative: independent blogs as well as social networks and social media such as Facebook[99], YouTube – where a 'Benetton Channel' was created the 24th February 2006[100] and Twitter[101] were involved and all perfectly integrated within the It's:My:Time website, http://casting.benetton.com/.

---

[97] "Instead of using professional models, we thought, why not ask the world to show us what they really look like -- instead of trying to show the world what we think it looks like" Andy Cameron, Executive Director of Fabrica, interviewed by Agnes Teh for CNN on February the 25th 2010. http://edition.cnn.com/2010/WORLD/europe/02/25/benetton.global.casting/index.html
[98] http://www.canneslions.com/work/media/index.cfm?award=99 at The Cannes Lions International Advertising Festival, Benetton with it's:my:time was one of the 19 finalists for the 'Best Use of Social Media Marketing'.
[99] http://www.facebook.com/benettoncasting. 17,626 People 'liked' the page as off September 27, 2010 while on November the 1st 2010 the likes were 19,557.
[100] http://www.youtube.com/user/benetton as off September 27th 2010, the channel had 1,610 subscribers and had been viewed by 626,157 individuals
[101] http://twitter.com/benettoncasting/, with 644 followers as off September 27th, 2010

The most interesting part of this contest was when an expert jury panel chose twenty individuals, among the one hundred winners announced on the 18th of March, and invited them – at Benetton's expense – to New York City to model for the company's 2010 fall/winter campaign[102]. The company also took care of inviting some of the most followed worldwide fashion bloggers to the shooting, in order to get a consistent coverage not only on print media but also on online media. The community that the contest had managed to create was updated on every development through the ad hoc YouTube channel.

The fall/winter campaign of 2010 is now ready and appears on the It's:My:Time official blog, on print media and in any Benetton store.

It's:My:Time was undeniably a success. Indeed, it was *such* a success, that it became a permanent initiative.

Figure 3.5 – IT'S MY TIME playbill.

- **The case of the Jewelry Based Luxury brand: Bulgari.**

The Italian jeweler brand Bulgari has been, since its creation in 1884, synonym of high quality and luxurious jewelry designs. Over the years, the company has gone public (1995) and expanded into new businesses, more or less related with its core product category, but always remained true to its opulent brand image.

In 2001 for instance, following a joint venture with Marriott International, the company formed a new luxury hotel brand 'Bulgari Hotels & Resorts'[103] while in 1997 it started producing leather fashion accessories[104]. This diversification process started in 1992, when the company entered the fragrances and skincare businesses with its

---

[102] http://www.benetton.com/alfresco/d/d/workspace/SpacesStore/f758038d-1472-4b93-aa46-7d7630320bc6/IT'sMyTimeNY_en.pdf

[103] http://www.bulgarihotels.com/home.html?param_id_lingua=1
[104] http://ir.bulgari.com/bulgarigroup/glance/

first perfume 'Eau Parfumée au Thé Vert' (one year later 'Bulgari Parfums' is indeed created).

Still, the company gets recognized mainly for its jewelry collections. One of the most famous ones celebrated its 10th anniversary this year. We are talking about the B.zero1 collection created in year 2000, which is, as of today, Bulgari's most sold collection with 1.4 millions pieces[105]. It's core piece, the B.Zero1 4-band ring in 18kt yellow gold, with its central spiral and the two lateral rims with the double logo 'BVLGARI BVLGARI' engraved, has become one of the brand most recognized and iconic products.

To update it, two new ring designs, based on the original B.Zero1 ring, were created[106]: the first has a central spiral made of ceramic –either in black or in white, while the second design was created with the help of a very special collaborator, the Indian sculptor Anish Kapoor[107]. 'Anish Kapoor B.Zero1 ring', in pink gold and steel, reminds indeed one of his most famous sculptures: the Chicago's Cloud Gate.

The anniversary was celebrated worldwide with different events.

In Italy, a party was thrown at the Bulgari Hotel in Milan. Instead of keeping the event exclusive, restricting the invitations to a limited number of the brand's 'friends' (celebrities, investors, partners, it-girls, luxury and fashion insiders and so on…), the brand decided to invite also the authors of the most followed Italian fashion blogs[108].

The latter were invited to a cocktail party the 19th of May 2010. The new B.zero1 collection was there for them to admire and to take pictures at. In return, the majority of them mentioned the event on their blog, thereby promoting (we will see whether unconsciously or not in the next chapter) Bulgari and its collection through online media[109].

Hence, Bulgari broke the rule of thumb that characterizes many Luxury and Fashion companies: Exclusiveness is indeed a prerequisite adopted throughout the whole communication strategy, so as to limit the dilution of the brand perceived image.

---

[105] http://www.marketwire.com/press-release/Bulgari-Celebrates-Bzero1-the-Epitome-of-Bulgari-Design-1266338.htm

[106] http://en.bulgari.com/department.jsp?cat=cat00035

[107] Anish Kapoor official website: http://www.anishkapoor.com/. One of his most known sculptures is the 'cloud gate'–also called the 'bean'- part of the Chicago's Millennium park.

[108] http://www.graziamagazine.it/moda/accessori/bulgari-la-presentazione-della-collezione-b-zero-1

[109] Two examples of blogs that wrote about the event: 'cool and contagious' http://www.coolandcontagious.com/search?q=bulgari and 'pigchic' http://www.pigchic.com/2010/05/31/bulgari-cocktail-party-zero1-collection/

It looks like the brand is becoming more prone to the use of online media, as it dedicated an entire new website to the collection (http://bzero1.bulgari.com/) as well as launching a special 'B.Zero1 iPhone Application'[110].

- **The case of the Ready-To-Wear High End Fashion brand: Roberto Cavalli**

'Roberto Cavalli' (RC) is an Italian fashion company founded in 1960 by the entrepreneur and designer Mr. Roberto Cavalli and his wife, Mrs. Eva Cavalli. It operates in the sector of Luxury apparel and fashion accessories for men (with the prêt-a-porter line 'Roberto Cavalli Uomo'), women (Roberto Cavalli Donna), youngsters (the diffusion lines Just Cavalli Donna and Uomo, launched in 1998) and children (Angels & Devils Collections created in year 2000. The last diffusion line for men and women was created in 2000, the 'Class' collection, which targets a consumer that is more attracted by classic shapes, patterns and designs. Roberto Cavalli is a highly diversified brand; its offering indeed ranges from clothing to perfumes, footwear, leather accessories, eyewear, swimwear, jewelry, vodka[111], wine, catering services[112] and underwear[113]. The company takes care only of the production of its prêt-a-porter line for women, outsourcing the rest to external manufacturers such as Gibò[114], Ittierre[115], Albisetti[116], Simonetta[117], Morellato&Sector[118], Marcolin[119] and Dressing[120].

The brand started using Internet as a new communication channel at the beginning of year 2009, successfully implementing a Roberto Cavalli official Blog (http://www.robertocavalliblog.com), a Twitter account

---

[110] http://www.socialmedianews.it/worldwide-launch-of-the-official-bulgari-b-zero1-iphone-app
[111] http://www.robertocavallivodka.com/
[112] The cavalli club in florence http://www.cavalliclub.com/ and the just cavalli club in Milan http://www.justcavallihollywood.it/
[113] http://www.robertocavalli.com/it/sitemap.do
[114] http://www.robertocavalli.com/it/companyProfile/mission.do
[115] http://www.ittierre.it/. Ittierre Spa has a licensing agreement with RC for the production of Just Cavalli Uomo and JC Donna.
[116] Albisetti Spa official website www.albisetti.it. Albisetti Spa produces underwear for all the brands of the company: RC Donna, RC Uomo, Just Cavalli Uomo and Just Cavalli Donna. It also produces ties for the RC Uomo line, beahcwear for the two Just Cavalli lines and foulards for RC Donna. http://www.milanofinanza.it/giornali/preview_giornali.asp?id=1650278&codiciTestate=10&sez=giornali
[117] Takes care of the production of the two children collections. http://www.simonetta.it/
[118] Produces jewelry and watches for RC. http://www.watchservicecenter.it/
[119] www.marcolin.com for eyewear.
[120] http://www.dressing.it/ for the two Class lines

(http://twitter.com/Roberto_Cavalli/status/21896117454) and Facebook page (http://www.facebook.com/album.php?aid=189124&id=342088343060&ref=mf).

It is precisely on this Facebook page that the last 4th of August, the brand launched a contest aimed at finding new 'creative fashion designers'[121]. Participants were asked to submit three menswear sketches, accompanied by a resume, together with "a cool soundtrack" describing what Roberto Cavalli's world is to them. The contest prize and assessing methods were a bit blurry; it was not explained who chose the winners, if it was be Roberto Cavalli's fashion team's decision only or if also the fans' opinion was taken into account, and neither was the kind of work opportunity that is offered to the winners.

The expiry date to apply to the contest was September 10, 2010. Five days later, the five finalists had to be announced on the Facebook page. Also the twitter account was used to incite people to participate[122].

- **The case of the Leather Goods Based Luxury Brand: Louis Vuitton.**

One last example of social media use by a Luxury company is that of Louis Vuitton *Malletier*, the French fashion house founded by Mr. Louis Vuitton, who entered the business of luxury *'malles'* (trunks) – and other leather goods – in 1854.

Today, Louis Vuitton is the most profitable and most known division of the holding company LVMH[123] – Louis Vuitton Moët Hennessy – that resulted from the merger of the former fashion house with champagne producer Moët et Chandon and cognac manufacturer Hennessy in 1987. LVMH indeed competes into five main business areas: fashion & leather goods, wines & spirits, perfumes & cosmetics, watches & jewelry and selective retailing. 'Fashion and leather goods' total revenues in 2009 amounted to 6 302 millions euros, nearly 37% of the Group total revenues for the same financial year (17 053 millions euros). Within the latter division, Louis Vuitton is the most known Luxury brand among the other thirteen brands owned by the group[124].

---

[121] http://www.facebook.com/RobertoCavalli#!/RobertoCavalli?v=app_128441167198955
[122] http://twitter.com/Roberto_Cavalli/status/22694438735
[123] http://www.lvmh.com/comfi/pdf/LVMH_PR_2009_UK.pdf.
[124] The other brands being: Loewe, Céline, Berluti, Kenzo, Givenchy, Marc Jacobs, Fendi, StefanoBi, Emilio Pucci, Thomas Pink, Donna Karan and Nowness.
http://www.lvmh.com/groupe/pg_societe.asp?str_table_1=societe&secteur=1&rub=3&srub=2

53

The company became famous over the years for its maniacal attention to quality and details (a common attribute of fashion companies) and for its trademarked (but still much copied and object of counterfeiting) canvases – in particular, the *Damier* canvas created in 1888 and the *Monogram* canvas created by the founder's son, George Vuitton in 1896, registered as a trademark in 1905.

Louis Vuitton is the luxury company *par excellence*: the purchase of its products automatically entitles the consumer to a certain social recognition[125] and its core values, as advertised on the company's official website, http://www.louisvuitton.com/, are in fact timelessness, permanence, exclusivity and inalterability. The products are the result of the most skilled craftsmen's accurate work, trained according to tradition. Louis Vuitton's offering is also produced exclusively in France (the only exception being footwear, which is produced in Italy) and their high quality is guaranteed by the use of the most rare and precious materials only. The fact that Louis Vuitton belongs to the luxury sphere is moreover proved by the brand expansion strategy over the years, from its core product – which was not apparel – to male and female clothing lines in 1998 (Marc Jacobs was and still is the appointed designer), scrapbooks (1998), fine jewelry (2001) and luxury watches (2002).

The company carefully chose the brand extensions to undertake (e.g. travel guides, luxury pens and rollerballs) so as to fuel the brand 'lifestyle' (which in the case of Louis Vuitton is that of the 'Journey') and to entitle customers to experience it.

Louis Vuitton joined Facebook on June 15, 2009 (according to what is reported on their official Facebook page http://www.facebook.com/LouisVuitton) and titled its official page 'The Art of Travel by Louis Vuitton'.

The page has been customized, in the sense that only four of the traditional main tabs were kept ('wall', 'info', 'photos' and 'videos') to which were added 'fashion show', 'Campaign'[126] 'Mon Monogram' and 'Legends'. The page has indeed been divided into seven principal areas that would reflect the company current initiatives, core values and offer.

The brand used the Facebook channel to broadcast its fashion show live on the Internet. The first show broadcasted was the Women Spring/Summer 2010, on the 7th of October 2009 (Figure 3.6).

---

[125] Even if in mature market such as Europe this is not anymore (at least in general) the main feature/ driver for the consumption of a luxury good

[126] The content of this area changes according to the period of the year.

The Art of Travel by Louis Vuitton Louis Vuitton is proud to announce the live online broadcast of its Women's Spring/Summer 2010 Ready to Wear collection on Facebook on October 7, 2009 at 2:30PM (Paris time) / 8:30AM EST.

Louis Vuitton is going one step further and confirming its digital intentions as the first luxury brand to offer a live broadcast of ...
See More

Louis Vuitton Women Spring/Summer 2010 Live Fashion Show on Facebook
Watch the Louis Vuitton Women Spring/Summer 2010 Fashion Show live on Facebook
Wednesday, October 7, 2009 at 2:30pm
www.facebook.com/LouisVuitton

October 1, 2009 at 6:04pm · Comment · Like · View Feedback (140) · Share

Figure 3.6

Two twitter accounts, reporting the same news published on the Facebook page, were simultaneously[127] launched: one for Louis Vuitton France http://twitter.com/louisvuitton_HQ with 26,388 followers (Figure 3.7), one for Louis Vuitton Japan, http://twitter.com/LouisVuitton_JP/followers, with 3,940 followers and one for Louis Vuitton US http://twitter.com/LouisVuitton_US with 131,590 followers - as off November the 1st, 2010[128].

Figure 3.7

All trace back to the brand's official website: http://www.louisvuitton.com/.

---

[127] The first tweet by Louis Vuitton http://twitter.com/LouisVuitton_HQ/status/2208439918

[128] Again, to give an idea of Social Media's use increase, followers back in October the 7th 2010 were: for the LV France account 24 053, 3 386 for the LV Japan and 123 408 for LV US. This means that in less than 1 month, followers for each one of the three accounts have increased, respectively, by 9.7%, 6.7% and 16.4%.

Finally, let's conclude this third chapter by providing some data retrieved through Scoutlabs[129], a searching tool that enables the companies using it to monitor what is being said about their brand[s] over the Internet in terms of volumes and in terms of 'on which social media is my brand most discussed' (do people talk about my brand more on Twitter or on Facebook?): Figure 3.8 shows the number of mentions registered on blogs, forums, Twitter and news over the last 6 months for two French Luxury brands, one that has embraced Social Media for a while now (Louis Vuitton) and one that has only recently started (Hermès); Figure 3.9 shows the same for four Italian ready-to-wear companies, two of which make large use of Social Media, while the other two have only a Facebook account open along with their official website; and Figure 3.10 shows the volume of mentions for the two most famous fast fashion retailers, Zara and H&M, compared with that of UCB.

These three graphs show how the fashion and luxury brands the majority of individuals aspire to 'in real life'[130] are – predictably – also the most discussed brands 'online'. This is indeed the case of French luxury company Hermès, of Italian prêt-à-porter company Prada and of Italian fashion house Valentino. None of these three companies has given great attention to social media. Yet, these latter are more discussed than some of their competitors who have, on the contrary, placed great emphasis on social media.

While this may give the impression of being a good reason for Fashion and Luxury companies *not* to use Social Media, the opposite is, in fact, true.

Luxury and fashion companies, precisely because of their peculiar communication strategy (a communication strategy that has to advertise products changing at least every six months, leveraging on aspirational values, on word-of-mouth and on buzz, whether it is through the use of celebrities, events or limited collections), are one of the most discussed topics on Social Media and should hence absolutely start using them, despite their skepticism[131].

---

[129] Scout Labs LLC, http://www.scoutlabs.com/about/, is a San Francisco-based company that created a monitoring tool/application reporting what is being said about a certain company on Twitter, Facebook, MySpace and even networking and blogging sites in foreign languages. The Scout search tool also rates the comments it finds as positive or negative. Coca-Cola co. is one of the company using it.
Needleman, S. E. (2009). *Relief for Twitter Headaches*. Wall Street Journal Online. http://online.wsj.com/article/SB10001424052970204683204574356441457884888.html
[130] (2008). *Consumers and Designer Brand* – a Nielsen Global Report. http://it.nielsen.com/site/documents/2008_GlobalNielsenLuxuryBrands_May08.pdf
[131]

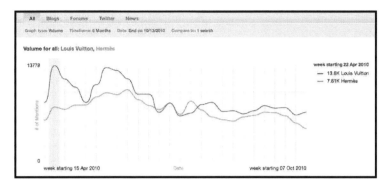

Figure 3-8 French Luxury Companies' Number of Mentions online over the last 6 months.

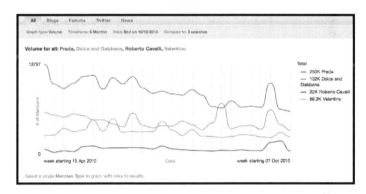

Figure 3-9. Italian high-end Fashion Companies' Number of Mentions online over the last 6 months

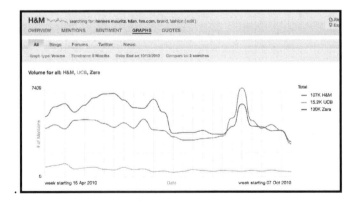

Figure 3-10 Mass Market Fashion Companies' Number of Mentions online over the last 6 months.

Chapter Four: Proving Social Media's crucial Role.

In the previous chapter, I tried to provide empirical qualitative evidence of Social Media's use by Fashion and Luxury companies. Let's now discuss the data and results described in the previous chapter as well as providing some additional quantitative information corroborating these considerations.

Paragraph 4.1: What emerges from the Cases presented in Chapter Three

Following what has been observed and reported hitherto, we can assert that:

- **Fashion blogs remain a tricky and little understood phenomenon.**

This is also what emerged after an investigation of this subject matter during the conference "Fashion Blogs: Sharing Creativity through Web 2.0?" held at the Università Cattolica del Sacro Cuore of Milan, the 28th of September 2010[132]. The round-table conference was aimed at discussing the main virtues and vices, drawbacks and benefits of fashion blogging within the Italian territory. There was a clear divergence of opinions: participants such as Francesca Giorgetti, fashion editor of Style.it[133] recognized that fashion blogs:

- o Enable the immediate 'registration' of the so-called 'street styles' and their sharing/publication on the Internet.

- o Created, with their websites' layouts made of 'posts', a new 'way' of presenting and sharing fashion-related news, that is being copied also by professional fashion journalists and by Fashion or Luxury companies whishing to open a blog or to update their official website's interface. This is for instance the case of French Fashion house Chanel with its official blog[134] constructed through

---

[132] The conference was held in Italian. Here is the homepage and program of the event
http://fashionblogsconference.wordpress.com/
[133] Style.it is the main website of Condé Nast the publishing company of magazines such as Glamour, Vogue and Vanity Fair.
[134] Chanel's Official Blog: http://chanel-news.chanel.com/en/

'posts'; of Italian Fashion company Max Mara which vested one of its press office's employee (Emilie) with the duty of updating the company's blog[135]; of Dolce&Gabbana online luxury magazine 'Swide' (the influence here is even more striking, since Swide was labeled a 'blogazine'[136]) or of Vogue.it, where the director, Ms Franca Sozzani, keeps a personal diary[137] that she updates daily.

○ Provide information with a high degree of specificity and futurity.

However, Ms. Giorgetti also severely described some fashion blogs as:

○ Indirectly contributing to the hampering of the Fashion and Luxury sectors' efforts in the battle against counterfeiting. Some fashion bloggers were indeed photographed with products that appeared as evidently counterfeited to the trained eyes of industry's insiders – but not to those of the average blog reader.

○ Being too auto-referential and thus uncritical.

○ Having uncritical followers – hence limiting space for improvement.

Luca Lanzoni, Elle Italia's fashion section editor, confirmed that blogs (along with Social Networks) have created a new language, a new direct channel through which consumers can directly relate to the company. They allow fashion magazines and companies to understand consumer's needs and to satisfy them in a more efficient way than before.

Hence, a first risk that fashion companies should avoid is that of hiring or collaborating with a fashion blogger external to the company who is not perceived as compatible, by consumers, with the Brand's Corporate Image and Values[138].

---

[135] Max Mara's official Blog: http://blog.maxmara.com/en/
[136] i.e. a magazine with the tone and personality of a blog. Swide website: http://www.swide.com
[137] 'Il Blog del Direttore': http://www.vogue.it/magazine/blog-del-direttore/2010/10/12-ottobre
[138] No unsuccessful collaboration between a fashion or luxury company and a blogger have been observed yet; however, in Italy, the weekly magazine 'Donna Moderna' received several critics for collaborating with a certain fashion blogger to report the Milan fashion week that took place in September 2010.

Especially when hiring a blogger who has been doing well on Internet for quite a while, the company should gather as much information as possible on the latter. Internet may be confusing, but one of its advantages (or disadvantages, depending on how one sees it) is that whatever was once shared through the Internet remains on it forever – literally.

- **H&M** correctly understood tha**t no matter the number of social media used, they all must be integrated within a domain belonging to the company itself.**

This is exactly what the company did through the implementation of its 'Social Media Room'.
Furthermore, the utilization of a fashion centered community blog – Lookbook.nu – within the media plan further advertised the Social Media Room, since the contest that was run on lookbook was shared on this area of H&M's official website. Other benefits engendered by this initiative were: an increase in Brand Awareness, a higher degree of intimacy with the online community and hence potential customers, a push to H&M's garments' use on Lookbook (through the gifting of vouchers to be spend solely at H&M's stores), the creation of new advertising material at zero costs (each week five participants were selected and their photos appeared on H&M's official website as part of the online advertising campaign) and, last but not least, a probable increase of H&M's items sold over the period the contest was held [139].

- **American Apparel took inspiration from the User Generated Content phenomenon to communicate with - and advertise its brand to - customers.**

One of the outcomes of the contest that the brand launched on lookbook.nu was indeed a catalogue made of participants' photos. Understanding that lookbook itself is 'an online catalogue of virtual outfits', the company undeniably selected the right venue where to launch the contest; lookbookers were indeed highly participative.
American Apparel also gained some economical advantage from this initiative: the booklet's content was in fact completely user generated, saving the company the costs of hiring professional models, photographers o photo editors and it was

---

[139] This hypothesis is not however provable since we lack official data, as for instance, the extra number of items sold worldwide , with respect to average, by the company retail channels over the period the contest was held, provided no other discounting initiatives have been undertaken at the same time.

moreover sold at a cost of $1 per piece on their official website. The fact that several hundreds of individuals participated guaranteed a heterogeneous and remarkable number of pictures from which to choose: it is doubtful whether the company would have been able to provide such a variety of 'outfits' in such a short period of time. Finally, by rewarding the 25 most hyped looks with a discount code to be used on the online shop of the brand, the latter was advertised and revenues where probably registered, since a purchase is necessary to use the discount code – which is dissimilar from, for instance, the voucher that HM gifted its contest winners with.

- United Colors of Benetton **used Social Media to set up its own casting agency, to create a new advertising campaign and to implement a 'window' entailing a direct and participative relationship with its customers.**

The company successfully transformed the search for 20 new models embodying the Brand Values (multiculturalism, colorfulness, originality and unconformity) into an online social instrument (the It's My Time official blog) aimed at improving the communication with existing and future customers.

UCB played the originality card, in the sense that it set up the very first advertising campaign where the models are not professionals, nor UCB customers, but simply individuals that, according to UCB, reflect the Brand's Corporate Values. This is a totally brand new type of advertising campaign. Hence, the main upsides were that the company certainly benefited from an increase in Brand Awareness, it renewed its relationship with clients, advertised the brand amongst the youngest (UCB had indeed lost some market share over the years to Fast Fashion retailers such as Zara or HM) and reduced the need of external players for what concerns the communication strategy – said need being already null due to the existence of Factiva.

As mentioned in the preceding chapter, this UCB initiative has become permanent, even if its was probably launched as an experiment. The 'It's My Time' blog plays therefore the role of UCB's official casting agency. By using this new channel, the company is certain of having an assured degree of novelty within its communication strategy (guaranteed by the diverse contribution of its multinational readers/participants) while keeping the traditional – aesthetical or not – codes characterizing it (this is ensured by the company setting up some precise boundaries through, for instance, the blog's layout or posting rules and by having the last saying over who is chosen).

- Bulgari was one of the **first Italian luxury brands to recognize the importance of channeling advertising information through blogs.**

It recognized how the latter often talk directly to possible and existing consumers. The company probably set certain conditions, i.e. invited the bloggers to the event asking them to later report it on their blogs, with photos and written descriptions of the new collection. This however clearly impedes bloggers to keep an unbiased opinion.

- Roberto Cavalli's example **confirms Facebook and contests as one of the most used methods to engage customers online.**

Facebook is indeed the first Social Network (the first type of social media) adopted by fashion and luxury companies as part of their media plan[140]. This is due to the fact that consumers rely significantly on their friends, family members and peers more than anyone else when it comes to making a purchase decision[141]. Moreover, by creating a Facebook account open to everyone instead of a group joinable only through an invitation, High-End Fashion and Luxury brands can build themselves a community. Although many of the 'fans' may not be able to afford their products, the Facebook page builds the "lust for the product", the idea of "one day I'll be able to afford that" which is, as we saw in Chapter One, a main component of luxury appeal. Finally, a daily updated Facebook page, with diverse type of content, such as videos, photos and event reports keeps customers engaged, since they can interact by commenting or 'liking' each update.

---

[140] Examples include Hèrmes or Cartier, which have started only recently to show some interest in the social media sphere and have hence opened a facebook account. Hèrmes' official facebook account: http://www.facebook.com/hermes. Cartier's official Facebook account: http://www.facebook.com/Cartier.

[141] (2010). Nielsen/Facebook Report: The Value of Social Media Ad Impressions. http://blog.nielsen.com/nielsenwire/online_mobile/nielsenfacebook-ad-report/
(2010). Understanding the value of a Social Media Impression: A Nielsen and Facebook Joint Study http://en-us.nielsen.com/content /nielsen/en_us/report_forms/Understanding-the-Value-of-a-Social-Media-Impression-A-Nielsen-and-Facebook-Joint-Study.html

For what concerns contests, they are one the most used forms of advertising through Social Media, since one of Social Media's main characteristics is <u>participation</u>. However some hints suggest that Roberto Cavalli's contest was not as successful as the company expected: the end date was moved forwards to the 10th of September (some other details were changed during the contest, like for instance, the number of sketches to submit[142]) and the personnel/staff in charge of the Facebook page had to incite people to participate several times.

- Louis Vuitton **had a clear Social Media strategy planned in mind when it entered the Social Media arena.**

The brand did not develop it as a simple 'experiment' but as <u>a long-term strategy that would foster and sustain the off-line communication strategy</u>. Through the use of Twitter and Facebook, Louis Vuitton successfully transferred and propelled its brand lifestyle into the Social Media arena. Naming the Facebook page 'the Art of Travel by Louis Vuitton', choosing Louis Vuitton's two most famous canvases color (brown) as the background color for the Twitter account and keeping the tone of voice of virtual communications 'formal' are all small (yet crucial) examples showing how the company succeeded in implementing <u>a coherent and consistent online communication strategy.</u> The Social Media used follow indeed the common thread, traditionally characterizing the company, that of 'the Journey'. We furthermore observe an alignment of communication codes.

We saw that Louis Vuitton has three different Twitter accounts, one for each of the three Triad's zones. In fact, the account 'Louis Vuitton HQ- Head Quarter' was implemented to address French and European clients (who represent together 29% of LVMH's), while the accounts 'Louis Vuitton US' and 'Louis Vuitton JP' were created to inform, respectively, United States (18%) and Japanese (18%) clients[143].

---

[142] Roberto Cavalli's contest winners:
http://www.facebook.com/album.php?aid=204348&id=342088343060
Roberto Cavalli contest Finalists:
http://www.facebook.com/album.php?aid=203258&id=342088343060
[143] LVMH's Fashion and Leather Goods'Revenues by geographical region of delivery in 2009
http://www.lvmh.com/groupe/pg_chiffres.asp?rub=2&srub=2. Unfortunately no official data was provided for what concerned 'louis vuitton fashion and leather goods' revenues'. The numbers reported here above refers also to other fashion brands owned by LVMH such as Givenchy, Kenzo, Marc Jacobs, etc.

This allows the company to provide each one of its most important markets with the right type of information (and customizing it when necessary – for instance, on the Japanese twitter account, news are reported in Japanese and not in English).

With the expansion of Luxury and Fashion companies in emerging markets such as China and India (Louis Vuitton entered China 18 years ago[144]) and Asia Pacific Internet use being dominated by Social Media[145], the brand should think about creating a specific Twitter account also for China[146].

Indeed, 80% of Chinese wealthy consumers are under 45, compared with 30% in the US and 19% in Japan[147]. This, combined with the fact that Asia is the region with the highest number of Internet users on the world[148] (825 millions) and that China, within Asia, is the country contributing the most to this number (Chinese internet users were indeed estimate to be 384 millions at the end of 2009)[149] means that, especially in emerging markets, Fashion and Luxury companies should absolutely avoid neglecting the new media communication channel.

Finally, as proved by Scoutlabs' searches, Social Media campaigns may not be sufficient to improve brand overall Online Awareness.

However, Social Media must still be used, if not to carry virtual campaign then, to monitor what is being reported/discussed by customers or the public opinion in general on the Web. It is clear that even those companies that do not desire to adopt Social Media will be obliged to do so, since their brand is already talked about through (and on) them (see figures 3.8, 3.9 and 3.10).

---

[144] *March 2010: The China luxury market is France's to lose.* China Economic Review's online article. http://www.chinaeconomicreview.com/cer/2010_03/Luxuriating.html
[145] (2010). Social Media Dominates Asia Pacific Internet Usage.
http://blog.nielsen.com/nielsenwire/global/social-media-dominates-asia-pacific-internet-usage/
[146] This delay may be due to the fact that Social Media are sometimes banned in China.
[147] Atsmon,Y., Ding, J., Dixit, V., St Maurice, I. & Suessmuth – Dyckerhoff, C. (2009). *The coming of age. China's new class of wealthy consumers.*
http://www.mckinsey.com/locations/greaterchina/mckonchina/reports/mcKinsey_wealthy_consumer_report.pdf
[148] http://www.internetworldstats.com/stats.htm
[149] http://www.internetworldstats.com/stats3.htm

Paragraph 4.2 Summing up Social Media's main Strong Points.

Hence the real – new – question that emerges is not whether Social Media use is necessary or not, since it clearly is; but rather *how* can a company successfully implement Social Media? How to ensure their efficient and effective execution?

This is indeed their main problem: since they are 'a new media', no rules are there to regulate their use. Social Media are truly inauspicious if and only if they are implemented without any kind of directives or instructions.

They should hence be subjected to all kinds of monitoring, supervision, control or inspection policies/processes scheduled for old media.

But how come there are no instructions for what concerns Social Media use?

After all, as we saw in Chapter Two, they have been around for quite a while now.

Two reasons may explain this occurrence:

First of all, no one foresaw Social Media's success as a business tool. Let us please remember that Social Media were born as a new way to share content through the Internet.

Secondly, just as any other Internet originated tool, Social Media is not considered 'real', as it is first and foremost 'a virtual thing' i.e. non existent. Hence, whatever was shared through Social Media was, for a long time –and still unfortunately is – considered as non-existent by far too many companies, and Luxury and Fashion companies make no exception. The most shared opinion regarding social media, back to 2008 or 2009[150] was in fact 'why should a virtual tool be regulated?'.

As a conclusion to this second paragraph, here is a list of six main reasons justifying the deployment of social media that yield to six precise benefits/strong points:

---

[150] Safko, L. & Brake, D. K. (2009) *The social media bible: tactics, tools, and strategies for business success.* 1st Edition. Hoboken. John Wiley & Sons. p.XV.

1. While television remains the uncontested sovereign of the media kingdom[151], the incredible rapidity at which Social Media are being adopted cannot be ignored anymore. The first main reason is indeed that Social Media's usage is undeniably increasing year after year (or rather, month after month) regardless of the geographical area[152], hence enabling the coverage of an important share of the market. Moreover, Social Media are becoming the favorite media of certain age brackets because of an increasing in Internet's access (as emerged from several researches presented in paragraph 4.3). By omitting the utilization of Social Media, companies are losing the possibility to address an audience that would be difficultly reached otherwise.

Hence, <u>thanks to Social Media, new markets and new audiences are contacted</u>.

2. <u>Social Media share any type of content – images, written documents and videos – *faster* than any other kind of communication media.</u>

This is in particular due to the fact that Social Media work basically on any type of mobile as well as on other types of portable hand devices.

The most striking example is the Twitter application that connects you to the Internet in real time – through a mobile phone. This microblogging application is perhaps the best instrument to magnify and intensify the **word-of-mouth** and amplify the resulting **buzz** that it may create. Facebook, on the other hand, is not as efficient in this latter aspect. However it provides a higher degree of **customization**, which is vital for a Fashion or Luxury company that desires to propel its brand into the digital era without compromising its soul.

[151] (2010). What Consumers Watch: Nielsen's Q1 2010 Three Screen Report.
http://blog.nielsen.com/nielsenwire/online_mobile/what-consumers-watch-nielsens-q1-2010-three-screen-report/
[152] (2010). What Americans Do Online: Social Media And Games Dominate Activity.
http://blog.nielsen.com/nielsenwire/online_mobile/what-americans-do-online-social-media-and-games-dominate-activity/
(2010). U.K. Web Use Up 65% Since 2007 – Social Networking more than Doubles.
http://blog.nielsen.com/nielsenwire/global/u-k-web-use-up-65-since-2007-social-networking-more-than-doubles/
(2010). Social Media Dominates Asia Pacific Internet Usage.
http://blog.nielsen.com/nielsenwire/global/social-media-dominates-asia-pacific-internet-usage/

3. If self-implemented, Social Media have very little, or rather nonexistent, implementation costs.

Their set up may result time-consuming in a first moment but certainly proves to be a time-saver in the long-run. For instance, what is the cost of creating a Twitter account? Of creating a Facebook account? Zero[153]. The main expense will be that required to create the platform where all the different Social Network will be integrated, i.e. the company official's website or blog. This cost is however null since basically any Fashion or Luxury company already has its personal website (what is more, traditional Luxury companies such as Hermès or Cartier already have a Facebook account as well).

This is a non-indifferent advantage for Luxury and Fashion companies, since communication costs in these sectors represent the largest chunk of total costs. In particular, more than 50 percent of a Fashion products' final price is generally set aside to cover these communication expenses. This is perhaps why Mr. Bernard Arnault refers to them – or more precisely to the Internet at large – as one of the three trends a company competing in the luxury industry should leverage on[154], the other two being perseverance and persistence on value(s) and retail control to avoid the occurrence of discounting policies (the advent of Yoox has already proved that making a product available online will not hurt the controlled offline distribution that characterizes luxury brands).

4. Social Media can indeed be all incorporated on your official website.

This means that through the use of Social Media you are indirectly pulling more people together on your website thereby ensuring a higher degree of visits (and probably of contacts in a second moment), with all the benefits that extra visits may engender. The individuals gathered on the company's Facebook or Twitter accounts generate a new flow that can be redirected to the group's or company's virtual Head Quarters, the Official Website.

---

[153] Of course, if and when social media monitoring is outsourced or carried through the use of a specific monitoring tool build by external professionals – like scout labs or radiant6 searching tools, some expenses are incurred.

[154] Friedman, V.(2009). *How to Manage the transition into quality* – Interview to Mr. Bernard Arnault. Newspapers' article. The Financial Times.

5. Social Media are the entrance gate to (firstly) local Social Network and (then to) global Social Networks.

By entering a social network through the use of Social Media, the company gives the possibility to its clients to review (and comment on): the business, the products, the collections, etc. This enables the creation of a certain degree of **intimacy** between the company and its best consumers.

6. At this point, one may ask, 'why should a Fashion or Luxury company, whose main characteristic is exclusiveness desire to connect directly with its clients?'. The first answer is, why shouldn't it? Exclusiveness is not synonym of low-quality services. Directly providing information to your clients is a moral duty and a service that any respectable company working in the Fashion and Luxury sectors should observe. The second reason is that discussions and information on a certain company are already 'out there on the web', whether the parent group or company wants it or not, as proved by the searches ran through the Scoutlabs' program[155]. Individuals are gathering on Social Networks and using Social Media to discuss the latest attributes of Miu Miu's 2010 S/S collection or the way Versace's last catwalk show was organized (for example).

Hence, Social Media grant the company object of these discussions the possibility to have a saying (or better said a certain control) over what is being said and written about it.

Social Media is a valid tool that improves **customer relationship management** and helps marketers understand how a product (or a certain marketing campaign) is perceived by consumers.

---

[155] www.scoutlabs.com

69

Paragraph 4.3: Why should Fashion and Luxury companies couple Social Media with Old Media?

Following what has been reported in paragraph 4.2, one may be tempted to ask 'why Social Media have not substituted Old media *yet*?'. The next paragraph is hence aimed at explaining, with a **threefold answer** why, after all what has been previously written, Fashion and Luxury companies should couple Old Media (and not substitute them) with New Media.

1. **Firstly**, and as seen in paragraph 4.2, let us stress Social Media' s essentiality. This is even truer if we consider that Internet's access (and consequently, Social Media's access) is exponentially growing worldwide. This is very interesting for this thesis because the greater the Internet access the higher will be the probability of using it, as well as that of using Social Media.

This seems to be at least Italy's case according to <u>an Audiweb[156] research</u> conducted on a sample N of 47 972 000 individuals (Italy's total Internet population ranging from 11 to 74 years old) over a period of nine months starting from the 14th of September 2009. In particular, the <u>following 3 outcomes</u> raise great interest:

- The possibility to access the Internet has increased by 10,4% with respect to last year, <u>with 67,7% of the total sample's population haven access to Internet from any type of locations</u> (at home, at work, at school, at a library, at an internet point etc.) through the use of any type of device (computer, PC or portable hand devices such as mobiles or IPads).

- <u>The use of PDA, smartphones and mobile phones has increased by 30,3% with respect to last year</u> (confirming The Nielsen company market research on the US population, reported in Paragraph 2.4, 'Mobile'). Nearly 10% of the sampling population hence accesses the Internet through the use of smartphones or similar

---

[156] Internet usage in Italy: Audiweb Trends, agosto 2010. *Sintesi e analisi dei risultati della Ricerca di Base sulla diffusione dell'online in Italia –VIII Edizione.* Dati cumulati cicli 3 e 4 del 2009 + ciclo 1 e 2 del 2010 dal 14/09/09 al 31/05/10.

portable hand devices. Many are indeed the fashion companies that have already issued some iPad applications[157].

-        The two age brackets with the greater access to the Internet are 'Teens', [11 – 17] with 84,6% of them having access to the Internet whenever and wherever and the one including individuals ranging from 18 to 34 years old, the so-called 'Net Generation' or '**Generation Y**', with 81,9%.

Still, as off now, Social media and Old media seem to address two different targets and to have two different ways of presenting content - a bit like Amazon's Kindle and paper books. The content is the same but the way it is displayed and showed is too different to compare the two. **This is the first reason for which a substitution of Old media by Social Media is not advisable**. The choice of which media to use is a **subjective decision**, depending on one's familiarity with technology and it is not strictly correlated to one's age; the world is plenty of adolescents preferring newspapers and books to blogs and kindles just as there are many people in their sixties that would rather update their blogs or vlogs[158] and consulting the online version of the financial times than reading a newspapers or a book on their couch.

The previously mentioned Audiweb research can help explaining why **older adults are using the Internet more than what is commonly thought**. Indeed, the top three motivations pushing Italians Internet users[159] to surf the web are: 'the Internet enables me to acquire information on any kind of subject/topic/issue' (46%), 'this is the fastest service I can profit from' (28,1%) and 'there are things that can be found only on the Internet' (25,3%); while the top two attributes providing satisfaction were: 'I found what I couldn't find somewhere else' (27,3%) and 'I found news/information that I could not find with other media' (21,3%).

The fact that the Internet provides information that are difficulty found somewhere else has **encouraged Internet's use also among those generations that have**

---

[157] Hay, S. (2010). *The best fashion apps for the iPad*. Financial Times' article.
http://www.ft.com/cms/s/2/1c3c5d4e-c1ea-11df-9d90-00144feab49a.html

[158] This is the case for instance of Peter, aged 83 years old, also known as 'Geriatric1927'on Youtube. Named 'The Internet Grandad' by The Daily Mail and The New York Times, Peter has a Youtube channel that he updates regularly: http://www.youtube.com/user/geriatric1927
[159] The answers were provided by the 25 563 000 individuals that actually surfed the Internet during the last month of August.

experienced the Internet for the first time as grown ups (i.e. all of those people born before 1970/1971 – indeed an individual born in those years reached major age the year internet was born, 1989). The commonly shared idea that individuals born before 1970 or 1965 – the young baby boomers – do not use Internet that often and should therefore be not targeted through online marketing strategies is hence counter argued by these Audiweb report's results

Many other have recently quarreled this commonplace. A second report conducted on the US population this year and published by the Nielsen Company[160], warns marketers to pay greater attention to the **baby boomers generation** (individuals born between 1946 and 1964, as seen in Table 4.1). Researches have indeed proved that baby boomers adopt new technologies with enthusiasm. This is very interesting, especially for Fashion and Luxury companies since baby boomers have been labeled as consumers with a high purchasing power and willingness to pay. Moreover, since the oldest are starting to retire next year, they will soon become the 'new seniors', a consumer segment that expects high level of quality but that is removed from aesthetic obligations – the perfect target for luxury companies.

A Third study disclosed by the Pew Research Center[161] reports in particular 2 results supporting what stated up here:

- *"Social networking use among Internet users aged 50 and older has nearly doubled—from 22% to 42% over the past year"*. This confirms the fact that while Social Media's use has increased significantly across all age groups, **older users have been particularly enthusiastic about embracing them**. Even though email continues to be the main tool used by baby boomers (to maintain contact with friends, family members and colleagues), many of them now rely on social network platforms to manage their daily communications (sharing links, photos, videos, news and status updates with a growing network of contacts).

---

[160] *Why Marketers Can't Afford to Ignore Baby Boomers.* (2010)
http://blog.nielsen.com/nielsenwire/consumer/why-marketers-can't-afford-to-ignore-baby-boomers/
[161] *Older Adults and Social Media Social networking use among those ages 50 and older nearly doubled over the past year.* (2010). http://pewinternet.org/Reports/2010/Older-Adults-and-Social-Media.aspx

-     "*Half (47%) of Internet users aged 50-64 and one in four (26%) users aged 65 and older now use social networking sites*" (such as Facebook and LinkedIn).

Internet users aged between 18 and 29 years old continue to be the heaviest users of Social Networking sites like Facebook and LinkedIn, with 86% saying they use the sites[162]. **However**, over the past year, their growth paled in comparison to that of older users: between April 2009 and May 2010, **Baby Boomers'** (Internet users aged between 46 and 64 years old, see Table 4.1) **use of a social networking site grew by 88%** and New Seniors' (individuals aged 65 and older) use increased by 100%, while the growth rate for those aged 18 to 29 years old (the Net Generation) was of 13% only.

Hence, old and rich[163] consumers (Luxury and Fashion companies' traditional clients[164]) are increasingly using the Internet and Social Media in particular as a result.

To conclude this first part of paragraph 4.3, here is Table 4.1, explaining which age brackets represent which generations. There are different ways of segmenting the population according to age brackets; for our part, we used a combination between the one defined by PSFK, a trends research and Innovation Company[165] and that of Audiweb:

---

[162] This confirms what reported in the Audiweb reserach.
[163] http://www.emarketer.com/Report.aspx?code=emarketer_2000430
[164] Atsmon,Y., Ding, J., Dixit, V., St Maurice, I. & Suessmuth – Dyckerhoff, C. (2009). *The coming of age. China's new class of wealthy consumers.*
http://www.mckinsey.com/locations/greaterchina/mckonchina/reports/mcKinsey_wealthy_consumer_report.pdf
[165] http://www.psfk.com/2009/02/us-report-internet-usage-by-age.html

Table 4.1

Year of Birth/Generations	Age in 1989	Age Today (2010)
[1993-1999] Pre Teens	Were not born yet.	[11 – 17]
[1977-1992] Net Generation	Not of major age yet.	[18 – 33]
[1965-1976] Generation X	Those born before 1971 are of major age	[34 – 45]
[1955-1964] Young Baby Boomers	[25 – 34]	[46 – 55]
[1946-1954] Old Baby Boomers	[35 – 43]	[56 – 64]
[1937-1945] New Seniors	[44 – 52]	[65 – 73]
Born in 1936 G.I. Generation.	53 years old	74 years old

However, observing how - and if - Social Media's use according to diverse age brackets changes is not enough to understand why fashion and luxury companies should couple social media with old media.

2. **A second reason** for which Social Media and Old Media should be coupled lies in the fact that many respectable magazines and newspapers (not only those writing about Luxury and Fashion) have indeed an online version aside from the paper one which is either identical or reports nearly all the same articles that are published on the paper version. **This means that Publishing companies are already coupling Old media with new/social media.** Vogue Italia for instance has an official website, http://vogue.it, a Twitter account with 10,302 followers http://twitter.com/vogue_italia[166] and a Facebook page with 145,402 'likes' http://www.facebook.com/VogueItalia. The same is true for Vogue UK[167] or Vogue France[168], Vogue Russia[169]. The only exception is Vogue US.

---

[166] Vogue Italia's director, Franca Sozzani, also has a personal twitter account that she uses for business purposes: http://twitter.com/francasozzani.
[167] Vogue UK's online version http://www.vogue.co.uk/, Twitter Account http://twitter.com/vogue_london and Facebook Account http://www.facebook.com/VogueUK.
[168] Vogue Paris (France) official website http://www.vogue.fr/, Facebook Page http://www.facebook.com/pages/Vogue-Paris/286292202704?v=app_121430634574025 and Twitter account http://twitter.com/vogueparislive
[169] Vogue Russia official website http://www.vogue.ru/, Facebook Page http://www.facebook.com/VogueRussia and Twitter account http://twitter.com/#!/VogueRussia

Newsmagazines recognized that their consumer base has changed its consumption behavior and have adapted consequently. They are aware of how certain 'readers' can only be 'captured' by being present on the Internet.

This is what their blogs and virtual versions are there for, to pool together more 'virtual visitors' by ensuring that a large amount of individuals reads the online version of the magazine they increase the probability of these people buying the paper version. The methods and tactics used are many – posting shorter articles on the online version to increase curiosity for instance. In fact, as showed by Table 4.2, the online versions of the main Italian fashion magazine gather definitively much more readers if compared to their paper version.

Table 4.2

Newspapers	Paper Version / Old Media – copies sold per month[170]	Online Version / New Media – unique users per day[171]	
Vogue italia	66 825	Style.it**	87 170
Vanity fair Italia*	266 030		
Glamour Italia	250 357		
Elle Italia	164 836	33.829	
Marie Claire Italia	159 235	10.966	
* This is a weekly magazine			
** Corresponds to Vanity fair, Glamour and Vogue magazines altogether			

Why? The reasons are very simple and obvious: as we saw at the beginning of this paragraph, millions of individuals surf the Internet every day. Moreover, information on the Internet is free, whereas these magazines are priced from a minimum of €1,90 (Vanity Fair) to a maximum of €5,00 (Vogue Italia).

3. **Finally**, many have erroneously addressed Social Media as a substitute of Old media because fashion bloggers, if compared to fashion journalists, were not subjected to a Brand's influence. The magazines for which fashion journalists work, as we saw in Chapter One, are indeed highly dependent on the advertising

---

[170] Data by Prima Comunicazione – for old media – monthly moving average over the period 1/07/2009 to 30/06/2010. http://www.primaonline.it/2010/09/27/83979/diffusione-dei-mensili-giugno-2010/
[171] http://www.audiweb.it/

Fashion or Luxury brands place on their pages and must often be careful about what they write when describing a catwalk show or collection[172]

This is not however true anymore, since many fashion bloggers have started advertising and weaving relationships with designers and fashion houses[173] thereby hampering the impartiality/neutrality of their opinions and of their fashion choices, without forgetting the other downsides of fashion blogging, as explained in paragraph4.1. **This is hence the third reason for which Old Media should not be substituted with New Media**.

[172] Severgnini, B. (2010). *Niente Critiche Alla Moda*. Newspapers' article. Il Corriere della Sera. http://www.corriere.it/italians/10_marzo_10/Niente-critiche-alla-moda_6aab526e-2bae-11df-8630-00144f02aabe.shtml

[173] Copping, N. (2009). *Style bloggers take centre stage*. Financial Times' article. http://www.ft.com/cms/s/2/89f8c07c-cfe0-11de-a36d-00144feabdc0.html

Conclusion

I started writing this thesis with the following research question in mind: "Are Social Media the new essential tool to be paired with Old Media for a Fashion and Luxury communication strategy to be successful?".

I immediately started my thesis by providing an exhaustive definition of the two main 'building blocks' of my hypothesis: in Chapter One I hence described the main characteristics of a Fashion and Luxury communication strategy (how is it carried out? What are its main peculiarities with respect to the communication strategy of a company belonging to a different sector?). The same was executed for Social Media in Chapter Two.

Having clarified the two main components of my Research Question, I proceeded with the testing of the latter.

Firstly with Chapter Three, where I provided some qualitative data, i.e. cases, showing how indeed Social Media have been increasingly used by Fashion and Luxury companies in the last couple of years (2009/2010). Reporting these cases was essential to set doubts aside. I tried to provide instances that were in fact observable to anyone surfing the Internet and that would hence mark the point.
However, as a student graduating from a genuinely University of Economics, I do recognize that nothing dispels doubt as much as the right numbers.
This is why the last and Fourth Chapter of my work has been dedicated to a critical analysis of the cases reported in Chapter Three and to the presentation of some quantitative data proving both the cruciality of Social Media within Fashion and Luxury's media plan and the necessity of coupling these latter with the so-called Old Media on which Fashion and Luxury companies have always highly relied for advertisement.

However, while there is no possibility of doubting that the answer to the initial research question is a positive one, it must still be noted that Social Media indispensability can be obstructed by the lack of instructions regarding their use. It is indeed advisable for any Fashion or Luxury company to adopt a certain set of regulations when implementing Social Media.

When launching the brand into the digital age, Fashion and Luxury companies should be very careful since the risk is that of compromising the brand's soul.

This means, for instance, that when creating a Twitter account, it would be preferable to create one that is clearly recognizable to the customers' eyes: by using core products or key symbols as a background image; by creating only one official twitter account and by clearly reporting the brand/company's name. If the designer or the CEO himself/herself desires to have a Twitter account, he or she obviously can and in some cases it is even advisable, since it can help sharing – for example – the designer's view on a collection or any other aspect of the company in the quickest and fastest way possible. However, he/she should remember to tweet only work-related and savvy comments.

One downside of the Internet is in fact that anything that is ever published on it remains on it even after it has been 'cancelled/deleted'.

Here is a list of **5 simple directives** a Fashion or Luxury Company could keep in mind when actualizing a social media strategy:

1. **Carry out a first analysis on the web aimed at understanding how often and when is [are] your brand[s] mentioned**. This means vesting some of your already existing employees (or hiring some new ones) with the duty of 'scouting' the Web. Some companies already have them and they are known as the 'truth squats' – generally groups of 2 or 3 individuals that scan the web searching for false rumors concerning their company or brand to intervene in real-time[174]. A specific monitoring tool, such as the one provided by the companies Scoutlabs[175] or Radian6[176] is recommended – and it would be even more advisable that the company develops one on its own.

2. According to what has been observed online (e.g. the brand name has bad associations[177]; the brand name is mentioned too little if compared to

---

[174] Needleman, S. E. (2009). For Companies, A Tweet In Time Can Avert PR Mess. Dow Jones & Company, Inc. The Wall Street Journal.
[175] http://www.scoutlabs.com/about/,
[176] http://www.radian6.com/
[177] For instance, I had to ignore the Italian fashion brand Gucci when carrying the searches on scoutlabs, because the latter was associated to an American singer named 'Gucci Mane' and results were distorted because of this homonymy. http://en.wikipedia.org/wiki/Gucci_mane

competitors; the brand name is mentioned often on some social media like Facebook, but not enough on forums or on Twitter - for instance) **set up the scope** (not really the geographical scope but rather 'on which social media to act') **and the goals of the strategy** (e.g. increasing the number of mentions per months of the brand; increasing positive associations with the brand and thereby fostering a positive brand image or most importantly, assessing what value – equity – the consumer places on our brand), **deciding which actions/activities must be carried out**.

3. Even if 'truth squats' are generally not very large, **set up responsibilities** (who is in charge of which activity), **the timetable** (when) **and the probable budget**.

4. **Execute** the strategy.

5. **Close the strategy and monitor feedback**. Has the situation changed? Did the corrective action work?

These **five** steps may vary according to whether Social Media are used at the Senior, Marketing, Public Relations or Human Resources/Sales levels.

At the Senior level, microblogging networks like Twitter – or an official blog – can help the company's opinion leader (the designer of a Fashion House or Apple's CEO), with a robust knowledge base, to build and raise awareness.

In a Marketing department, Social Media like YouTube foster the creation of new channels through which the company can share new content and carry promotions, thereby building more traffic.

For what concerns the Public Relations branch, inspecting the public's comments on YouTube, Facebook or Twitter, makes the company aware of what consumers are saying about their products, services and initiatives, enabling it to respond to possible complaints, thereby strengthening customer support and retention.

Finally, at the Sales/Human Resources levels, making use of Social Media such as LinkedIn or Facebook facilitates 'social recruiting' (i.e. locating and hiring new employees through the Web) and improves the company's ability to carry business intelligence and to create new networks.

As one may notice, the five steps aforementioned certainly do not form an original list of elements. On the contrary, they essentially represent the basic planning strategy used to set up any kind of project.

Still, many companies that have been using Social Media for a while now, have failed to follow the basic steps they would never dream of omitting for any other kind of 'real' project.

The absence of regulations when it comes to Social Media lies in them connecting 'virtual people'. Many marketers find it difficult to set up online marketing strategies through the use of Social Media that must address individuals nicknaming themselves 'luxuryismylife' or 'Ilovehautecouture' (just inventing here). Yet, these are 'real individuals', with money to spend and aspirations to leverage on.

Fashion and Luxury companies better start playing the game now, especially if we consider how Social Media's main features, as explained in the last chapter, allow a company to:

-     <u>Assess its current brand equity</u>, i.e. the value consumers place on its brand
-     <u>Impact said brand equity</u> (the ultimate goal of any communication strategy).

<u>Brand equity or value assessment</u> (1) is easily carried through Social Media rather than through Old media. Programs such as Scoutlabs not only measure the volume of mentions of a brand, they also specify 'of what kind' are the sentences the brand was worded in. This is an interpretation of sentiment analysis. By using a natural language processing that picks up on emotional key words or phrases (such as 'sexy' 'beautiful' 'love/loved/loving' 'enjoy/enjoyment' 'sad' ' recommend' etc), the software is capable of depicting whether the brand was mentioned by a consumer feeling love or hate, if he or she was making a wish, recommending one of the brand's products or complaining about a certain problem he or she is having - associated to the brand. Scoutlabs also recognizes six different types of quotes: love quotes, hate quotes, recommend quotes, issue quotes and caveat quotes and it is capable of measuring the overall general 'sentiment' associated over a certain period of time to the brand by the Internet audience through the use of 'sentiment graphs', which show the

volume of positive brand's mentions compared to the volumes of negative brand's mentions over a certain period of time.

Social media not only can assess the current brand value of a brand, but can also affect the latter (2).

Let us remember that Keller's model of Brand Image (1993)[178] states that Brand Equity derives from Brand Knowledge, which for its part derives from the combination of Brand Awareness and Brand Image.

Throughout this thesis, we have asserted and described many times how Social Media have had an effect on Brand Awareness. They are indeed helpful in providing a brand with a strong exposure (especially when compared to old media, as we saw in Table 4.2), thereby increasing Brand Recognition and are just as efficient in building up strong product category associations (Facebook and twitter are particularly effective in this) that will trigger the consumer's memory in the future and hence guarantee Brand Recall. For what concerns Brand Image (the perception that consumers have of a certain brand and of what it does for them), Social Media take part in sharing and communicating it but also have an impact over it, especially when they are used as a monitoring tool for customer service.

Brand Image is indeed certainly fostered when, for instance, the official Twitter or Facebook account of the company is utilized to answer a publicly visible online complaint, made by another Facebook or Twitter user about the brand. With one action, two results are obtained: the consumer whose complaint was taken into account will feel satisfied and will probably prove to be more loyal in the future, while the 'customer-support action' remains online for anybody to see it.

This means that Social Media have an indirect impact on Brand Knowledge and, as a consequence, also on a Brand's overall Value.

---

[178] Keller, Kevin Lane (2003). *Brand Synthesis: The Multidimensionality of Brand Knowledge*, Journal of Consumer Research, 29 (4), 595-600
Keller, Kevin Lane (1993). *Conceptualizing, Measuring, and Managing Customer-Based Brand Equity*, Journal of Marketing, 57 (January) 1-22

To Conclude, in this thesis we tried to prove:

1. Social Media's ability in creating Added Value. By talking directly to customers[179] and engaging them directly by granting them the possibility to participate in interactive initiatives, Social Media provide customers with an 'added value' that enhances and transforms the so-called 'Brand Experience' (the fact that consumers buy a certain branded product because it satisfies their particular needs and tastes) into 'Brand Engagement', where consumers buy a certain branded product because they *feel* a certain *emotional* attachment to the brand. This 'transformation' is rendered possible by the fact that Social Media (if and when well implemented) improve and foster customer brand loyalty and satisfaction (as explained on paragraph 4.1 from p.61 to p.65 and on the fifth point of paragraph 4.2 at p.69) by offering both online and offline experiences and new kind of services.

2. Social Media's decisive help to Fashion and Luxury companies facing the next generational shift. From 2009 to 2010, Social Media's use by US baby boomers has indeed increased by 88%, that US New Seniors by 100 % (as seen on p. 72) while the Generation Y is, along with the Teens Generation, the one making the heaviest use of social networking sites (as seen on p.71 and p.73).

3. Social media's crucial role in emerging market. As seen in the last part of paragraph 4.1 on p. 65, Asia Pacific Internet use is being dominated by Social Media. China in particular is the country with the highest number of Internet users within Asia.

Interestingly enough, the three Social Media's upsides stated up here retrace (plus or minus and in a more modest and synthetic way), the conclusions disclosed during the last Luxury and Fashion Insight report carried by the consulting company Bain & Company the on the 18th of October 2010 for the Fondazione Altagamma[180].

---

[179] Binkley, C. (2009). *From the Runway to Your Laptop; In Milan, European Labels such as Dolce & Gabbana Embrace the Digital Age*. The Wall Street Journal Online.
[180] D'Arpizio, C. (2010). *Altagamma 2010 Worldwide Markets Monitor*. Bain & Company. Powerpoint presentation.
http://www.altagamma.it/admin/contenuti/allegati/amministratori/altagamma/news/materiale%2018%20ottobre/MonitorAltagamma2010.pdf

I hope that while this thesis was aimed at showing Social Media's crucial role within a Fashion and Luxury's communication strategy, I was able to stress enough their main upsides to make it plain that their role is always vital, regardless of the industry or company's department they are employed in.

Bibliography

A

Atsmon,Y., Ding, J., Dixit, V., St Maurice, I. & Suessmuth – Dyckerhoff, C. (2009). *The coming of age. China's new class of wealthy consumers.* http://www.mckinsey.com/locations/greaterchina/mckonchina/reports/mcKinsey_wealthy_co nsumer_report.pdf

Audiweb Trends, agosto 2010. *Sintesi e analisi dei risultati della Ricerca di Base sulla diffusione dell'online in Italia –VIII Edizione.* Dati cumulati cicli 3 e 4 del 2009 + ciclo 1 e 2 del 2010 dal 14/09/09 al 31/05/10.

B

Benetton, A. Interviewed by Burrows, T. (2010). Benetton's It's My Time: casting the net. Newspapers article. The Daily Telegraph. UK. http://www.telegraph.co.uk/fashion/7482435/Benettons-Its-My-Time-casting-the-net.html

Binkley, C. (2009). From the Runway to Your Laptop; In Milan, European Labels such as Dolce & Gabbana Embrace the Digital Age. The Wall Street Journal Online.

Bulbarelli, P. (2009). *Milano, moda e tecnologia a braccetto.* Corriere della Sera's article. http://www.corriere.it/spettacoli/speciali/2010/moda/notizie/moda-tecnologia-sfilate-diretta-web_16d945d2-20bf-11df-a848-00144f02aabe.shtml

C

Cailliau, R. & Gillies, J. (2000). *How the Web was born.* 1st Edition. New York. Oxford University Press Inc.

Cirillo, A. (2007). *Armani, un regalo a Milano.* Newspapers' article. La Repubblica's online database. http://ricerca.repubblica.it/repubblica/archivio/repubblica/2007/02/20/armani-un-regalo-milano.html

Consumers and Designer Brand – a Nielsen Global Report. (2008). http://it.nielsen.com/site/documents/2008_GlobalNielsenLuxuryBrands_May08.pdf

Copping, N. (2009). *Style bloggers take centre stage.* Financial Times' article. http://www.ft.com/cms/s/2/89f8c07c-cfe0-11de-a36d-00144feabdc0.html

Corbellini, E. & Saviolo, S. (2009). *Managing Fashion and Luxury Companies.* 1st Edition. Milan. Etas.

Corcoran, C. T. (2006). *Blogging for bags - A growing group of writers is chatting up accessories.* Women's Wear Daily. Copyright 2006 Fairchild Publications, Inc.

Costolo, D. (2010). Tweet post. http://twitter.com/exectweets/status/15705793585.

D

Di Bari, V. (2007). *Web 2.0 : Internet è cambiato. E voi? : i consigli dei principali esperti italiani e internazionali per affrontare le nuove sfide.* 1st Edition. Milan. Il Sole 24 Ore.

E

Elad, J. (2008). *LinkedIn® For Dummies®.* Hoboken. Wiley Publishing Inc.

F

Ferdi, D. & Serlenga, L. (2008). *Alla corte di re Moda.* 1st Edition. Milan. Salani Editore

Fitton, L., Gruen, M. & Poston, L. (2010). *Twitter® For Dummies® 2nd Edition.* Hoboken. Wiley Publishing Inc.

Fontanelli, R. (2008). *Web, accessori e design le tre sfide di Ferragamo.* Newspapers' article. La Repubblica's online database.
http://ricerca.repubblica.it/repubblica/archivio/repubblica/2008/10/27/web-accessori-design-le-tre-sfide-di.html

Friedman, V.(2009). *How to Manage the transition into quality* – Intervew to Mr. Bernard Arnault. Newspapers' article. The Financial Times.

G

Grossman, L. (2006). *Time's person of the Year: You.* Newspaper' article. Time Publications. USA. http://www.time.com/time/magazine/article/0,9171,1569514,00.html

H

Hass, N.(2010). *Earning Her Stripes.* The Wall Street Journal Online.
http://magazine.wsj.com/features/the-big-interview/earning-her-strips/

Hay, S. (2010). *The best fashion apps for the iPad.* Financial Times' article.
http://www.ft.com/cms/s/2/1c3c5d4e-c1ea-11df-9d90-00144feab49a.html

K

Keller, Kevin Lane (2003). "Brand Synthesis: The Multidimensionality of Brand Knowledge," Journal of Consumer Research, 29 (4), 595-600

Keller, Kevin Lane (1993). "Conceptualizing, Measuring, and Managing Customer-Based Brand Equity," Journal of Marketing, 57 (January) 1-22

L

Laningham, S. (2006). *DeveloperWorks Interviews: Tim Berners-Lee.* Blogpost/Interview.
http://www.ibm.com/developerworks/podcast/dwi/cm-int082206txt.html.

M

March 2010: The China luxury market is France's to lose. China Economic Review's online article. http://www.chinaeconomicreview.com/cer/2010_03/Luxuriating.html

McCullagh, D. & Broache, A. (2007). *Blogs turn 10--who's the father? Blogging has been around for about a decade now--depending on how you define it and whom you ask.* CNET News.com, (c) CNET Networks Inc.USA.

N

Naomi, Eva e Claudia: la moda fa spettacolo. (2009). Newspapers' article. Il Corriere della Sera publications, http://archiviostorico.corriere.it/2009/settembre/26/Naomi_Eva_Claudia_moda_spettacolo_co_7_0909263069.shtml

Needleman, S. E. (2009). For Companies, A Tweet In Time Can Avert PR Mess. Dow Jones & Company, Inc. The Wall Street Journal.

Needleman, S. E. (2009). *Relief for Twitter Headaches.* Wall Street Journal Online. http://online.wsj.com/article/SB10001424052970204683204574356441457884888.html

Nielsen/Facebook Report: The Value of Social Media Ad Impressions. (2010). http://blog.nielsen.com/nielsenwire/online_mobile/nielsenfacebook-ad-report/

O

Older Adults and Social Media Social networking use among those ages 50 and older nearly doubled over the past year. (2010). http://pewinternet.org/Reports/2010/Older-Adults-and-Social-Media.aspx

Olins, A. and Bannerman, L. (2009). *New York Fashion Week to host catwalk show without the catwalk.* Newspapers' article. Times publications. http://women.timesonline.co.uk/tol/life_and_style/women/fashion/article5622399.ece

O'Reilly, T. (2010). *Six Years in The Valley.* Interviewed by The Economist during the economist 'Innovation Event' held in Berkeley. Audio format found at: http://video.economist.com/index.jsp?fr_story=7c533c16196b81c7fb025dde3688dfd34626dda0

O'Reilly, T. (2005). *What is Web 2.0.* Blogpost. http://oreilly.com/web2/archive/what-is-web-20.html.

O'Reilly, T. & Musser, J. (2006). *Web 2.0: principles and best practices.* 1st Edition. USA. O'Reilly Media.

P

Pavone, L. (2010). *Social Media e Editoria Online: relazione virtuosa o pericolosa?* Power Point presentation. IAB seminar.

Pearlman, L. & Abram, C. (2010). *Facebook® for Dummies® 2nd Edition.* Hoboken. Wiley Publishing Inc.

R

Riva, G. (2010). *Che cos'e' un social network: la fusione tra reti reali e reti virtuali.* Power point presentation. http://www.scribd.com/doc/27103243/Che-cos-e-un-Social-Network.

S

Safko, L. & Brake, D. K. (2009) *The social media bible: tactics, tools, and strategies for business success*. 1st Edition. Hoboken. John Wiley & Sons.

Sahlin, D. & Botello, C. (2007). *YouTube™ for Dummies®*. Hoboken. Wiley Publishing.

Schiro, A.M. (1997). *Designers' Council Opens Door a Bit*. The New York Times' article. http://www.nytimes.com/1997/12/09/style/designers-council-opens-door-a-bit.html.

Severgnini, B. (2010). *Niente Critiche Alla Moda*. Newspapers' article. Il Corriere della Sera. http://www.corriere.it/italians/10_marzo_10/Niente-critiche-alla-moda_6aab526e-2bae-11df-8630-00144f02aabe.shtml

Social Networks/Blogs Now Account for One in Every Four and a Half Minutes Online (2010). http://blog.nielsen.com/nielsenwire/global/social-media-accounts-for-22-percent-of-time-online/

Social Media Dominates Asia Pacific Internet Usage. (2010). http://blog.nielsen.com/nielsenwire/global/social-media-dominates-asia-pacific-internet-usage/

T

Terdiman, D. (2004). *Photo Site a Hit With Bloggers*. Blogpost. http://www.wired.com/culture/lifestyle/news/2004/12/65958. Wired.

The Connected Devices Age: iPads, Kindles, Smartphones and the Connected Consumer. (2010). http://blog.nielsen.com/nielsenwire/consumer/the-connected-devices-age-ipads-kindles-smartphones-and-the-connected-consumer/

U

U.K. Web Use Up 65% Since 2007 – Social Networking more than Doubles. (2010). http://blog.nielsen.com/nielsenwire/global/u-k-web-use-up-65-since-2007-social-networking-more-than-doubles/

Understanding the value of a Social Media Impression: A Nielsen and Facebook Joint Study. (2010). http://en-us.nielsen.com/content /nielsen/en_us/report_forms/Understanding-the-Value-of-a-Social-Media-Impression-A-Nielsen-and-Facebook-Joint-Study.html

W

Warren, C. (2009). LinkedIn surpasses 50 millions users. Blogpost. http://mashable.com/2009/10/14/linkedin-50-millon/.

What Americans Do Online: Social Media And Games Dominate Activity. (2010). http://blog.nielsen.com/nielsenwire/online_mobile/what-americans-do-online-social-media-and-games-dominate-activity/

What Consumers Watch: Nielsen's Q1 2010 Three Screen Report. (2010). http://blog.nielsen.com/nielsenwire/online_mobile/what-consumers-watch-nielsens-q1-2010-three-screen-report/

Why Marketers Can't Afford to Ignore Baby Boomers. (2010)
http://blog.nielsen.com/nielsenwire/consumer/why-marketers-can't-afford-to-ignore-baby-boomers/

Wilson, E. (2009). *Bloggers Crash Fashion's Front Row*. Newspapers' article. The New York Times.

Wunsch-Vincent, S. & Vickery. G. (2007). Participative Web: User-Created Content. Report prepared as as part of the WPIE work on Digital Content. Published on the responsibility of the Secretary-General of the OECD http://www.oecd.org/dataoecd/57/14/38393115.pdf.

Z
Zuckerberg, M. (2010). *500 Million Stories*. Blog Post
http://blog.facebook.com/blog.php?post=409753352130.

Websites

www.albisetti.it

http://www.americanapparel.net

http://www.anishkapoor.com

http://www.audiweb.it/

http://barracudalabs.com

http://www.benetton.com

http://www.benettongroup.com/en/

http://blog.cnc-costumenational.com/

http://www.bloglovin.com/

http://blog.maxmara.com/en/

http://blog.nielsen.com/nielsenwire/

http://www.bulgarihotels.com

http://www.canneslions.com/

http://www.cavalliclub.com/

http://chanel-news.chanel.com/en/

http://www.cheapmonday.com/about

http://www.chinaeconomicreview.com

http://www.corriere.it

http://www.dressing.it/

http://www.economist.com

http://edition.cnn.com

http://en.bulgari.com

http://en-us.nielsen.com

http://en.wikipedia.org

http://www.emarketer.com

http://www.fabrica.it/

http://fashionblogsconference.wordpress.com

http://www.ft.com

www.garancedore.fr

https://www.google.com

https://www.google.com/adplanner

http://www.graziamagazine.it

http://www.hm.com

http://www.independent.co.uk

http://www.internetworldstats.com/stats.htm

http://ir.bulgari.com/

http://it.nielsen.com

http://www.ittierre.it

http://www.linkedin.com

http://lookbook.nu

http://www.louisvuitton.com

www.ludicorp.com

http://www.lvmh.com/

http://magazine.wsj.com

www.marcolin.com

http://www.mashable.com

http://www.marketwire.com

http://www.milanofinanza.it

http://monkiworld.com/

http://www.nytimes.com

http://www.observer.com

http://www.oecd.org

http://online.wsj.com

http://www.oreilly.com

http://www.oreillynet.com

http://pewinternet.org

http://www.psfk.com/

http://www.primaonline.it

http://www.radian6.com/

http://www.repubblica.it

http://www.robertocavalli.com

http://www.robertocavalliblog.com

http://www.robertocavallivodka.com/

http://www.scoutlabs.com/

http://www.simonetta.it

http://www.socialmedianews.it

http://www.swide.com/luxury-magazine

http://www.telegraph.co.uk

www.thesartorialist.com

http://www.thestylerookie.com/

http://www.time.com

http://twitter.com

http://www.vogue.co.uk/

http://www.vogue.fr/

http://www.vogue.it/

http://www.vogue.ru/

http://www.watchservicecenter.it/

http://www.weekday.se/

http://www.wired.com

http://www.xe.com

http://www.youtube.com